MY COUNTRY
AND THE WORLD

Also by ANDREI D. SAKHAROV

SAKHAROV SPEAKS

MY COUNTRY AND THE WORLD

Andrei D. Sakharov

Translated by Guy V. Daniels

Vintage Books

A DIVISION OF RANDOM HOUSE

New York

Contents

To Foreign Readers
of <u>My Country</u>
<u>and the World</u>

My Country and the World is addressed to my com-
patriots who are re-examining critically their country, its
place in the world, and its future. It is also addressed to
foreign readers—to Western political leaders involved in
the complex and contradiction-ridden process of détente
and to the ordinary man in the street who is usually
remote from politics, who knows about life in the socialist countries only from his newspapers, and who feels
that what goes on there is not his business. But this sense
of isolation is an illusion.

Everyone's future depends on the way in which relations among the First, Second, and Third Worlds evolve,
and these relations in turn depend on the character of
these three segments of mankind. Of additional importance, there is a universal moral responsibility to use a
single standard in judging human misfortune and injus-
tice wherever they may occur.

I look to my Western readers for continuing attention
to the life of the socialist countries and for lively personal
interest in the defense of human rights. In particular, I
rely upon world opinion to support the idea of a political

amnesty in our country. Now, in the era of détente and after the European Security Conference at Helsinki, it has become more realistic to speak of this. The resolutions of the Conference embody significant obligations with respect to freedom of conscience, freedom to exchange information, and other human rights. All countries, including the USSR, have a vital stake in the fulfillment of these obligations, since international confidence and the fate of the whole process of détente depend in large measure on them. As yet, two months after the Conference, there has been no change in either the general or the human-rights policies of our country's leaders. I still hope that persistent attention to the principles proclaimed by the Conference will sooner or later bear fruit.

I appeal to my Western readers to keep this watch. I want to stress the paramount importance of defending particular individuals. In this book I have mentioned some of these people: Leonid Plyushch, whose mind is being destroyed in a special psychiatric hospital; Mustafa Dzhemilev, who is threatened with a fourth term of imprisonment; Bukovsky, Gluzman, Lyubarsky, Paulaitis, Khaustov, Superfin, Vins, Shumuk, and hundreds more. There is Vasily Romanyuk, who has been sentenced to a second ten-year term for his religious beliefs and for uttering a few compassionate words about Valentin Moroz. There are the members of Amnesty International, Sergei Kovolev and Andrei Tverdokhlebov, who have been arrested and are awaiting trial. There is the writer Mihajlo Mihajlov, convicted in Yugoslavia. Recently, after the Helsinki Conference, the publisher of the *samizdat* journal *Veche*, Vladimir Osipov, was convicted for the second time and sentenced to eight years in a labor camp.

Finally, I want to emphasize another thesis of my book. Everyone in the West should support Western unity and strength in the face of the totalitarian threat while at the same time encouraging balanced disarmament and close cooperation with the Second and Third Worlds.

I have written this book believing in the reason and goodness of mankind.

Andrei Sakharov
September, 1975

Publisher's Introduction

Born in 1921, the son of a Moscow physics professor, Andrei Sakharov was graduated from Moscow University in 1942. He was employed as an engineer in a war plant until 1945 and then joined the research group headed by the physicist Igor Tamm.

From 1948 to 1968 Sakharov worked on the military applications and later on the peaceful uses of thermonuclear reactions. After solving several crucial theoretical problems in the successful race to beat the Americans to the H-bomb, Sakharov was elected a full member of the Academy of Sciences in 1953 and was awarded three Orders of Socialist Labor, the Soviet Union's highest civilian award. Soviet leaders took particular pride in Sakharov's scientific accomplishments because he was a Russian, educated in Soviet, not tsarist or foreign, schools.

Realizing the danger of radioactive contamination, Sakharov began a determined campaign in 1957 to halt nuclear tests. (The accounts of Sakharov's interventions and Khrushchev's responses in *Sakharov Speaks* and *Khrushchev Remembers: The Last Testament* largely coincide, but differences in emphasis are noticeable.) In 1958 Sakharov argued in favor of intensive and continuous training of talented pupils in physics and mathematics, a position that conflicted with Khrushchev's call for two or more years of practical work in factories or fields prior to higher education. In 1964 Sakharov attacked the lingering influence of Lysenko's pseudo-scientific theories, which had resulted in the persecution of talented Soviet biologists and in the distortion of Soviet genetics, a science in which Russians had once excelled.

Venturing beyond purely scientific concerns for the first time, Sakharov cosigned a 1966 letter to the Twenty-Third Party Congress warning against the re-habilitation of Stalin. In the same year he protested the introduction of a new law against anti-Soviet slander that has since been used to jail many dissenters for non-violent expression of their beliefs. Sakharov considers 1966 as the year in which he ceased to identify himself with the Soviet "establishment," when he moved toward the role of independent public critic of the régime, the traditional role of the Russian intelligentsia.

In 1968 a Dutch correspondent telephoned from Moscow to Amsterdam the complete text of Sakharov's first book, *Progress, Coexistence, and Intellectual Freedom,* which had begun to circulate in *samizdat.* When a portion of the essay was published in the *New York Times* Sakharov gained sudden international fame even though he continued to refuse to meet with foreigners because of the secrecy restrictions placed on his scientific work. *Progress, Coexistence, and Intellectual Freedom* was a sober, reasoned, and humane plea for the rapprochement of the Soviet and Western blocs, based on demilitarization; the free exchange of information;

and international cooperation to share the benefits of scientific progress and to avoid its dangers—nuclear catastrophe, pollution of the environment, suppression of the individual personality.

Soviet-American détente owes much to Sakharov's first essay. There had been earlier discussion of convergence and détente, but Western public opinion, and especially Western scientists, began to take détente more seriously and to investigate the possibilities for disarmament and for Soviet-American cooperation after the appearance of Sakharov's essay. Henry Kissinger responded to Sakharov's essay by writing: "The Sakharov document is a deeply moving testimony to the freedom of the human spirit. It is therefore one of the most important documents on Communist affairs in recent years."

Several ideas from *Progress, Coexistence, and Intellectual Freedom,* ideas that seemed naïve at the time, have since become generally accepted. Sakharov called for a cooperative economic and technical assistance program for the developing countries; a moratorium on the construction of antimissile systems; international cooperation to prevent irreversible contamination of the environment and exhaustion of the earth's resources; informed public opinion and popular control of government as the only effective checks on the abuse of state power; a cooperative instead of a competitive approach to international relations.

The reforms of the Khrushchev era, the 1968 "Prague Spring," the stirrings of the Russian intelligentsia had encouraged hopes that the Soviet leaders might welcome fresh ideas. The military occupation of Czecho-slovakia, new arrests of Soviet dissenters, and the cancellation of Sakharov's clearance for his scientific work (in August 1968) dispelled this optimism. Sak-harov also suffered a personal loss in the death of his wife. The disruption of his public and private lives accelerated the evolution of his views. Relieved of his former responsibilities and the restrictions of secret work, Sakharov was free to learn more about ordinary Soviet life and to meet a wider circle of people, al-though two more years passed before he overcame his earlier inhibitions and began to make contact with cor-respondents and visitors from the West.

Two young Moscow physicists, Valery Chalidze and Andrei Tverdokhlebov, who had "published" *samizdat* responses to Sakharov's essays, were among his new acquaintances.* Their shared interests in physics and human rights led Sakharov, Chalidze, and Tverdokhle-bov to found the Moscow Human Rights Committee in November 1970. Despite harassment by the authorities, this unique association, which was independent of party or state control, succeeded in affiliating with interna-tional human rights organizations. The Committee's

---

* The disproportionate number of physicists, mathematicians, and other scientists in the human rights movement is partially explained by the greater job security accorded to scientists, and their privileged position in Soviet society. More important, only scientists are trained in classical logic, in the dispassionate ob-servation and analysis of facts. Soviet politicians, lawyers, his-torians, etc., are taught the method of justifying a predetermined conclusion—not the best schooling for the critical appraisal of official policy or for defending clients in court.

regular Thursday night meetings, with their discussion of civil rights topics relieved by occasional competition in scientific riddle-solving, seemed a bright beginning. But the very existence of the Committee aroused expectations that strained this fragile creation. More and more Soviet citizens looked to the Committee or to Sakharov personally for help in righting the wrongs they had suffered: Crimean Tatars deported to Central Asia in 1944; political prisoners reeducated by hunger; collective farmers without internal passports and thus deprived of the right to seek other work; Jews seeking to emigrate to Israel; Ukrainians hoping for cultural autonomy. Although the original conception of the Committee had been that of a study group, not an organization to provide legal aid in specific cases, Sakharov felt a moral obligation to respond to the pleas received from so many quarters. He spent hours and days composing appeals on behalf of Amalrik, Bukovsky, Plyushch, and scores of others, and then dictated them on the phone to foreign correspondents. He collected signatures on petitions to abolish the death penalty and to establish a general amnesty. He attended political trials when he could gain admission, or he stood outside, keeping vigil with other dissenters, when he was barred from the courtroom. On one of these occasions he met his second wife, Elena Bonner, a physician from Leningrad who had been active in the defense of Eduard Kuznetsov.

In February 1973 Sakharov was attacked for the first time in the Soviet press: the editor of the *Literary Gazette*, Alexander Chakovsky, accused him of "playing the fool" and of being influenced by "compliments from the Pentagon." In August an intense campaign was mounted against Sakharov and Solzhenitsyn. A distinction was made in the attacks against these two targets: Solzhenitsyn was identified as an enemy of the Soviet people, while Sakharov's earlier contributions to Soviet society were acknowledged and his political statements were attributed to the naïveté of a scientist led astray by the West's flattery. Forty fellow members of the Academy denounced Sakharov's views. A letter from Philip Handler, president of the U.S. Academy of Sciences, warning of the potential consequences to Soviet-American scientific cooperation, may have contributed to the rather abrupt termination of the anti-Sakharov campaign in September 1973.

Reprisals were then directed against Sakharov's family and friends. After the scientist called for an end to Soviet intervention in the Arab-Israeli October War, two "Arab terrorists" broke into Sakharov's apartment and threatened his family with violence if he did not keep silent. Elena Bonner was interrogated about the Western publication of Kuznetsov's *Prison Diaries*. She stated that she had helped to send out the manuscript while denying that this action constituted a crime. Bonner's children were barred from Soviet institutes yet were refused exit visas to continue their studies at Massachusetts Institute of Technology. Sakharov's associates in his human rights work were either arrested or forced into exile. Those who had publicly defended him lost their jobs or suffered other extra-juridical reprisals.

Depressed by the persecution of his family and friends, Sakharov considered accepting an invitation to spend a year at Princeton University. He initiated tentative inquiries concerning his eligibility for a passport, asking for assurances that he would be permitted to return to the USSR after a year abroad. In December 1973 Sakharov and Elena Bonner both entered a Moscow hospital; he because of high blood pressure and a heart condition, his wife because of a thyroid problem.

After their release from the hospital in January 1974, the authorities did not pursue the threatened criminal proceedings against Elena Bonner, and Sakharov did not finalize his plans for a visit abroad. The arrest and expulsion of Solzhenitsyn in February intensified the pressures on Sakharov. He was now the only dissenter with a major international reputation still active in Moscow.

A relative calm prevailed in the spring of 1974. Sakharov and his wife took a vacation in the south, where he wrote an article on the scientific and technological trends of the next fifty years for *Saturday Review*. When in Moscow Sakharov attended a weekly seminar at the Lebedev Institute of Physics. But as the year progressed, there was evidence that the human rights movement was still functioning and was capable of new initiatives: in May the *Chronicle of Current Events* resumed publication after a lapse of eighteen months and in the fall the first Amnesty International group in the USSR was registered. On October 31, at a press conference held in Sakharov's apartment, letters and appeals from Soviet political prisoners were circulated to foreign correspondents, and Sakharov renewed his plea for an amnesty. This bold step, reinforced by a special edition of the *Chronicle of Current Events* devoted to conditions in Soviet prisons and labor camps, may have triggered a new campaign by the authorities to suppress dissent and, in particular, to cut the ties between Soviet dissenters and their Western sympathizers. From 1973 Sakharov had been in touch by telephone with correspondents and friends in the West; after December 10, his calls from abroad were cut off although his local service continued to function. In December Sakharov received a letter containing threats against Elena Bonner's son-in-law and grandchild. There were numerous searches and interrogations in dissenter circles, culminating in the arrest of two of Sakharov's friends: the biologist Sergei Kovalev on December 27 and Andrei Tverdokhlebov on April 18, 1975.

Elena Bonner's failing vision was a constant concern. After two refusals, the Soviet authorities in July 1975 granted her permission to travel abroad for medical treatment. In June, Sakharov himself had been ordered to rest in his dacha because of a new heart condition. Despite all these worries, he found time to write *My Country and the World,* in which he returns, after seven eventful years, to the themes first formulated in *Progress, Coexistence, and Intellectual Freedom.*

While both essays share common concerns, Sakharov's views have evolved in several important respects. *Progress, Coexistence, and Intellectual Freedom* was addressed in the first instance to the Soviet leaders. *My Country and the World* is directed primarily to a

Western audience. Sakharov has come to understand that the state monopoly of information, press, and all means of communication blocks any direct appeal to Soviet public opinion and that the current Soviet leadership is not interested in reform but in preserving the status quo. The authorities effectively isolate dissenters from contact with Soviet society even without jailing them, although that option always remains available. But publicity in the West can serve a double purpose: the Soviet leaders show an erratic but pronounced sensitivity to the Western press and to the opinions of Western politicians and businessmen, and shortwave broadcasts from the West reach millions of Soviet citizens.

Roughly half of *My Country and the World* is devoted to comment on Soviet life and domestic problems, while the first essay concentrated on international problems. *My Country and the World's* assessment of the Soviet system differs radically from a statement in Sakharov's first essay: "We have demonstrated the vitality of the socialist course, which has done a great deal for the people materially, culturally, and socially and, like no other system, has glorified the moral significance of labor."

In *Progress, Coexistence, and Intellectual Freedom* Sakharov's main intention was to promote Soviet-American rapprochement and thereby avert the danger of a nuclear holocaust. Now that significant steps have been taken toward Soviet-American détente, Sakharov's main concern is the unity of the West. He believes that only informed, intelligent leadership can preserve the West's heritage of democratic government, its respect for the rights and liberty of the individual. The Soviet Union needs trade and technology from the West in order to overcome persistent deficiencies in its economy and in its scientific research programs. Firm Western insistence on its traditional standards will gradually induce the USSR to appreciate the benefits of responsible international conduct. The Western countries must overcome their competitive instincts and develop a united approach in their dealings with the USSR, demanding, in return for long-term credits and Western technology, effective verification of disarmament agreements, compliance with international treaties, and respect for generally accepted human rights. Sakharov fears that if the West does not hold to its course, the totalitarian practices of the Soviet Union will eventually undermine and bring about the collapse of Western institutions.

MY COUNTRY
AND THE WORLD

Prologue

The contours of the most serious and urgent problems facing the world today began to emerge and first became apparent to me and many others of my generation in the years following World War II.

Thirty years ago a bloody and most destructive war had just come to an end, leaving in its wake a sea of human misery on so vast a scale that its traces still persist. Famine raged over extensive regions of the planet, claiming millions of lives and threatening to spread further. Science and technology were laying the foundations for the "green revolution" which was supposed to curb that dread calamity. But scientific progress was also bringing nearer another danger for mankind— ecological catastrophe. Only a few individuals then realized the magnitude and imminence of this new peril.

The H-bomb did not exist. But the atomic bomb

already cast its shadow over the world, and for the first time mankind was facing the possibility of total annihilation. In Hiroshima and Nagasaki radiation victims were dying every day.

The fires of civil war had broken out in China. Stalinism had taken hold of the socialist countries and the bodies and souls of millions were being crushed in its terrible grasp. The furnaces of Auschwitz had gone out. But thousands were perishing daily in the frozen mines of Kolyma, Norilsk, and Vorkuta and in Stalin's countless "death brigades."* The number of Gulag victims had already reached the enormous total of 20 million.

In those years, public-spirited and penetrating thinkers—physicists and mathematicians, economists, jurists, public figures, and philosophers—advanced ideas occasioned by their profound anxiety for the fate of mankind. They included Einstein, Russell, Bohr, Cassin, and many others who anticipated the problems of our day, even though they did not understand many things concealed from the West by the Iron Curtain.

They called for the defense of human rights throughout the world, for national altruism, for the realization of an open world. (In explaining this concept, Niels Bohr emphasized that nothing should inhibit the exchange of information or freedom of movement.) They called for demilitarization, for aid to underdeveloped countries, for strengthening the UN, for world government.

---

* Construction projects using convict labor. [Translator]

Prologue

Even at that time I managed to find out about Bohr's statement. But it was only twenty years later, at the height of the 1968 "Prague Spring," that after many years of experience, of associating with notable individuals, of meditation, I decided to publish an article whose basic thrust was inspired by those ideas. The article, later published as a book, was called "Thoughts on Progress, Peaceful Coexistence, and Intellectual Freedom."* It was widely read, especially in the West, as one of the first statements of its kind from the mute inner recesses of the socialist countries. And to this day I have not basically changed the views I formulated at that time. But the many dramatic international events of the intervening years, conversations with people from my own and other countries (which have meant a great deal to me), and the widening of my personal experience have had their effect. Today I feel called upon to return to the themes of "Thoughts," emphasizing not the "optimistic futurology"—that is, the dream—but the dangers, illusions, and dramas of today: everything that stands between the dream and reality.

I want to stress at the outset that I should like to see, in this new phase of the relations between the capitalist and socialist countries that has been called détente, the realization of ideas which I cherish. And in fact there have been great changes for the better—at least in the style of political dialogue and to some degree in more

* Published in English as *Progress, Coexistence, and Intellectual Freedom*. Reprinted in *Sakharov Speaks*, New York, Knopf and Vintage, 1974. [Translator]

substantive areas. At the same time, a definite gap has opened between words and deeds, and the chances for the revival of dangerous illusions have increased. All this requires open discussion unfettered by diplomatic conventions or by conformism of the Eastern or Western type.

As was the case seven years ago, I fully realize my lack of competence in complex matters of societal relations. But I hope what I have to say will be useful nevertheless.

Conversations with foreign guests who visited me recently: with a group of American scientists who had come to the USSR for unofficial talks about the SALT agreements, and with Senator James Buckley of the United States—the first American statesman who considered it feasible to meet with me—helped inspire this book. During my meeting with Senator Buckley, which was very important to me, we discussed questions of foreign policy and certain domestic problems. I decided to set forth in writing the issues we had discussed. But I write slowly and with difficulty. This process dragged on for seven months, and that period witnessed some new and crucial events which are reflected in this book.

I have divided this book into several chapters:

I. Soviet Society. It is precisely the failure to understand what is hidden behind the Soviet façade and the potential dangers of Soviet totalitarianism that explains the many illusions of the Western intelligentsia and, in the final analysis, the amazing miscalculations and defeats of Western foreign policy, which without a struggle is yielding one concession after another to its partner in détente.

II. The Freedom to Choose One's Country of Residence. This important right is of great significance to all societies, both as a guarantee of many other basic rights and as a guarantee of international trust and of the openness of a society. The events surrounding the amendment to the trade bill passed by the US Congress reflected the attitudes of the socialist and Western worlds toward that problem—their tactics, principles, and deployment of forces. These events displayed the West's divisiveness, disorganization, and lack of information. I hope, however, that the future will show the West's firmness and its ability to learn from difficulties. The freedom to choose one's country of residence has become a test case—a proving ground for the whole style of détente.

III. Problems of Disarmament. Saving mankind from the threat of thermonuclear destruction undoubtedly takes priority over all other problems. But this task cannot be separated from other problems of a political, economic, humanitarian, and ethical nature—and above all from the questions of the openness of a society, of international trust, and of overcoming the disunity of the West. Any real solution to the problem of disarmament must include: a) a perfected system of verification, including inspections; b) a reduction of armaments, on the basis of parity, to a sufficiently low level (this refers both to negotiations on limiting the strategic weapons of the superpowers and to regional negotiations); c) elimination of the factors contributing to the arms race; d) elimination of the factors fostering strategic instability.

IV. Indochina and the Middle East. No one is yet able to fully evaluate the significance and scope of the tragedy of Indochina. But without question that tragedy became possible, to a considerable degree, because of the universal blindness with respect to the purposes and methods of those forces behind the young men who were thrown into the inferno of war. It is important that this lesson not be wasted. It is the duty of honest people everywhere to give all possible aid to the refugees and children who have suffered because of the war, not to commit another act of betrayal of the kind perpetrated against the displaced persons of thirty years ago.

V. The Liberal Intelligentsia of the West: Its Illusions and Responsibilities. Despite the many dangerous illusions that have become common currency among the intelligentsia, I believe that inner honesty, reason, and good will can prevail in this influential and most socially-conscious stratum of Western society.

The world needs demilitarization, national good will and internationalism, free exchange of information, freedom of movement, government disclosure of information, and the international defense of social and civil rights. The countries of the Third World must receive comprehensive aid. For their part, they must assume their share of responsibility for the world's future, devote more attention to production, and stop their speculation in oil.

These are the necessary conditions for overcoming the disunity of mankind—for saving it from the danger of thermonuclear destruction, famine, ecological catastrophe, and dehumanization: the conditions precedent to eliminating the dangers of scientific and technological progress and using it for the common weal.

This book was written under conditions of growing tension due to international and domestic developments and events in my personal life. I am indebted to those friends who helped me, and to the publisher. The generous support and help provided by my wife was of particular importance. It enabled me to carry the project through to its conclusion despite all the burdens of our life—misfortunes, illnesses, and threats.

I

Soviet Society

The life of our huge country is of course very complex
and multifaceted. As in any country, people's labor
(although not always productive or intelligently organized), and the increasing utilization of scientific
achievements and natural resources, are in one way or
another bearing visible fruit. Thousands of lively people, apparently satisfied with their lot, scurry about the
foothills of the trim skyscrapers of the New Arbat,*
which soar into the sky above Moscow. But behind this
façade is concealed (as, for that matter, in other countries besides ours) a great deal not visible to the
outsider. What is hidden is a sea of human misery,
difficulties, animosities, cruelty, profound fatigue, and
indifference—things that have accumulated for decades

---

* A street in Moscow. [Translator]

and are undermining the foundations of society. In our country there is an unusually large number of unfortunate people: solitary old men with small pensions; persons who never made a life for themselves—who have no job or opportunity to study or decent (even by our poor standards) housing; chronically ill men and women who cannot get into a hospital; a multitude of drunkards and individuals gone to seed; a million and a half prisoners—the victims of a blind and frequently unjust judicial machine that is the corrupt creature of the authorities and the local "Mafia"—who have forever been excluded from normal life; and simple failures, who did not manage to bribe the right person at the right time. It is virtually impossible to help all of them. And few try to do this in a general setting of an exhausting struggle for subsistence among the majority of the population, a surfeited, self-satisfied exclusivity among the minority, and an ostentatious and inefficient class structure. The desperate besiege the waiting rooms of important officials, from which many of them (especially the annoying ones) are taken straight to psychiatric hospitals.

I am very fond of the landscape and culture of my country and of its people; and I am in no way eager to play the role of a "debunker." But I feel it necessary to call attention to those negative aspects that are of basic importance to international relations and to an understanding of the situation in the country but that are passed over in silence by Soviet and pro-Soviet propaganda.

One "dogma of the faith" that has always figured in Soviet and pro-Soviet propaganda is the thesis of the uniqueness of the Soviet political and economic system, which (it is claimed) is the prototype for all other countries: the most just, humane, and progressive system, ensuring the highest labor productivity, the highest standard of living, etc.

The more obvious the complete failure to live up to most of the promises in that dogma, the more insistently it is maintained. The facts do not compare favorably with the developed capitalist countries; so the need to prop up this dogma, and the hypnosis of blind belief, are among the causes of the secretiveness of Soviet society. Many people can remember variations on this theme. Why should we learn from others? After all, we're ahead by a whole historical era. But in its turn, the secretiveness of society contributes to a great many negative phenomena in both domestic life and foreign affairs. For decades, great violence was committed under the banner of this faith in a unique world goal—a violence that Western liberals failed to notice: some out of naïveté, others out of indifference, and still others out of cynicism. One tragic example of this was the politicization of an intelligent and sincerely humanitarian writer who deliberately shut his eyes to the crimes of Stalinism (and some were evident even then), regarding the USSR as the only alternative to Nazism. Earlier, another writer declared that the rumors of famine in the USSR were exaggerated. "Nowhere have I eaten so well as in the USSR," he said, at the very time that NKVD "anti-profiteer" detachments* were machine-gunning starving children who were trying to cross the border. Vestiges of this blindness still exist, and in our time they have become more dangerous for the West itself. Today an understanding of the real nature of Soviet society—of what is concealed behind the respectable façade—is needed in order to appraise almost any problem of world significance.

In my opinion, contemporary Soviet society can be concisely characterized as a society based on state capitalism; that is, a system differing from contemporary capitalism of the Western type by virtue of complete nationalization, a Party-State monopoly of economic affairs—and therefore in culture, ideology, and the other basic aspects of life.

This opinion is apparently shared by a great many people both abroad and in the USSR—although in most cases the latter of course do not voice it. When, two years ago, I expressed myself in this spirit in an interview with Olle Stenholm, a correspondent for Swedish radio and television, that opinion was one of the chief pretexts for attacks on me in the Soviet press. And Stenholm's visa was quickly revoked. But in fact what I had said was almost trivial.

As many authors have noted, a complete state monopoly inevitably entails servitude and compulsory

---

* *Zagraditelnyye otryady:* detachments formed to combat the "bagmen" or petty grain speculators in the countryside in the early decades of the Soviet régime. The term also has a strict military meaning ("block-the-way detachment"), but the former interpretation is more likely here. [Translator]

conformism. Each person is completely dependent upon the state. In periods of stress this servitude engenders terrorism, and in calmer times it encourages a bungling bureaucracy, mediocrity, and apathy.

I want to describe first the economic and social aspects of Soviet society, then the ideological, cultural, and jurisprudential aspects, and finally the manifestation of our society's traits in international relations.

Without question, we do not have the world's highest labor productivity, nor is there any hope of overtaking the developed capitalist countries in the foreseeable future. What we have is a permanent militarization of the economy to an unprecedented degree for peacetime —something that is burdensome for the population and dangerous for the whole world. What we have is chronic economic stress: a lack of reserves despite all our natural resources—the black-earth belt, coal, crude oil, timber, diversity of climate—and despite a low density of population.

It is especially significant that with resources like ours, after fifty-eight years of gigantic efforts, including thirty years of uninterrupted peace, we have nothing even faintly resembling the world's highest standard of living. A worker from any developed capitalist country —not just the United States but also, say, France, West Germany, Italy, Switzerland, etc.—would not consider working for the kind of wages we pay or with our level of protection of workers' rights. In the USSR the minimum monthly wage is 60 rubles, and the average wage is 110 rubles. In terms of purchasing power, that minimum wage amounts to about $30 a month, or 150 new French francs, while the average wage amounts to about $55 or 275 francs.* Compare these figures with American standards: The average monthly wage is $600 to $800 per month; and a monthly income of $400 for a family consisting of father, mother, and two children is the official poverty threshold. For lower income levels, the state provides special benefits that a Soviet citizen would not even dream of. In other countries—like France, Italy, or West Germany—the wages are somewhat lower than in the United States, but the cost of living is also lower. In the USSR, people who live on their wages spend most of them on food. If he were to read about this, an American worker—who as a rule spends no more than 25 percent of his wages on food (of much better quality), and whose wife does not have to work if she doesn't want to—would no doubt find it wildly improbable.

Today the world press is full of items about inflation, the fuel crisis, and growing unemployment in the capitalist countries. I shall not analyze here the complex and diverse causes of these phenomena (among which the disorganizing factor of Soviet economic and general

* I have, perhaps somewhat arbitrarily, taken the dollar as equivalent to 2 rubles, which would probably make the purchasing power of the ruble somewhat greater than it actually is. I have used the price ratio in the case of foodstuffs (the chief expense item of the Soviet urban dweller), but without taking into account the vast difference in quality. In the Soviet Union, foodstuffs that are good by foreign standards are sold only in the private markets and at prices that are double state prices, and even higher. In the case of clothing, footwear, and other manufactured goods, the dollar–ruble price ratio is closer to one to four than to one to two.

political activity is by no means the least), nor do I want to underestimate their far-reaching psychological and political consequences. But I should nonetheless like to say: You are not dying of hunger; you don't have your backs against a wall. Indeed, even if you reduced your standard of living to one fifth of what it is, you would still be better off than citizens of the world's wealthiest socialist country.

In the face of the terrible threat of totalitarianism's advance, and the possibility of ecological catastrophe, it is very important that the bulk of the population, workers and businessmen, accept some temporary sacrifice in their living standards. Western civilization must gain some room to maneuver economically. This is essential first of all to the defense of Western civilization itself, and to the defense of ethical and democratic values throughout the world.

The low wage level in the USSR is especially burdensome for most white-collar workers: teachers, medical workers, and engineers. As a rule, they have no private garden plots; nor do they possess the "outside" sources of income (often quasi-legal) that are vital to many people.

How, then, does the state spend the huge sums that accrue to it thanks to artificially lowered wages? A considerable portion of this money is channeled into the expansion of production. But an equally large share goes into gigantic military expenditures; into financing covert and overt activities in all parts of the world, from the Middle East to Latin America; into providing a higher standard of living for the privileged strata of society; into paying for the costly blunders of the bureaucratic style of management. A certain portion of the revenue accruing to the state is put back into social needs—in particular, into pensions, medical care, and education—which thus can by no means be considered free.

On the social plane, it is very important to note the following:

First, we have short vacations, two weeks for most workers, which are scheduled at the discretion of management. (In France there are two vacations, winter and summer, with an overall length of four weeks.)

Second, we work a forty-one-hour week; that is, longer than in most Western countries.

Third, there is an absence of any real right to strike or to make organized appeals to higher authority. For years the Murmansk fishermen have been struggling against ruthless short-changing on their pay accounts, and trying to avoid paying bribes for permits to ship out. But so far the only result has been the victimization of a great many of the protesters: They have been fired, confined in psychiatric hospitals, and arrested. The campaign to improve industrial safety in mines and chemical plants has proved equally difficult. Safety measures are sadly neglected at many of these enterprises.

Fourth, we get very low pensions and benefits, even after several substantial increases under Khrushchev and Brezhnev. If we exclude "special" pensions and military pensions, the maximum monthly stipend is 120 rubles ($60), while the average is half that. Pensions for members of collective farms were introduced only recently, and they are very small. The pension for the loss by death of a head of a household is not paid if he committed suicide. Despite repeated increases, the benefit for mothers of large families (introduced during the war) covers only a small part of the expenses for raising children. Single mothers (without large families) receive a benefit amounting to 5 rubles per month for each child.

Fifth, every year, a number of Sundays or Saturdays are declared to be working days. The so-called Communist Saturdays are formally regarded as voluntary, but just try not going to work! The pay for those days is put into the state fund. Sunday, May 4, 1975, was designated a working day, and a day of paid vacation was lost. No one dared to protest except for two priests, one of whom was arrested.

Sixth, for most of the population, housing and daily living conditions remain bad, despite the large-scale housing construction under way in many cities.

It is not true that we have the cheapest housing in the world. Expressed in units of average wages, the cost per square meter is not lower than in most of the developed countries. For a family to obtain its own apartment is a piece of good luck for which many people wait all their lives. The usual apartment building is multistoried, with many apartments, and externally resembles a low-income project in America, though it has fewer conveniences and is more crowded. A separate room for each member of the family is something found only among a tiny percentage of the population. Except in a few "elite" cities, foodstuffs and manufactured goods are insufficiently available. The bread is of low quality, and contains additives. The meat situation is even worse. In most areas one has to stand in line for hours to get meat, and the quality is not always satisfactory even for dogs.* There is a serious and complete lack of electricity and gas. The water situation is bad. Most cities and towns still do not have a modern sewage system.

Seventh, the quality of education is low, especially in the rural areas. The classrooms are dimly lit and overcrowded. Organized transportation for children living far from school, so common in the West, is lacking almost everywhere. Arrangements for feeding the children are bad. The concept of free education is not extended (as it is in many nonsocialist countries) to

---

* In thousands of villages and small towns, people form lines in front of food stores the first thing in the morning, waiting for the bread to be delivered. They also hope that something else will be "tossed out" to them; and if that happens to be a scarce item like dried cod, the whole district gets in line. Even during the season of most intensive farm work, people (mostly women) sit or stand in front of the stores for many hours a day. The urge to work the soil—an internal stimulus that was still dominant among the peasant women and men forty years ago—has now vanished, along with material incentives. And half-drunk and totally-drunk men and youths, including a great many teenagers, spend whole days staggering through the squares in front of the stores. In the meantime the old women who are quietly gossiping say, "In the old days, the men and boys didn't drink like that—mostly just on the holidays."

providing children with food, school uniforms, and textbooks. The formal requirements involve complex and extensive programs of study that exhaust the students, and many hours of homework. But actually the intellectual level of education is very low. There are many deliberate injustices concerning the admission of students to college and graduate school. Among them, discrimination against Jews is especially well known. But there is equally unjust discrimination against students from rural areas, against members of the intelligentsia, the children of dissidents, of believers, of persons of German origin, and in general against all those who do not have connections.* The deterioration of the educational system is proved by the growing anti-intellectualism of society.

Eighth, medical care for the majority of the population is of a low quality. It takes half a day to get to see a doctor at a clinic. And what can the doctor do or understand in the ten minutes he has for seeing each patient? The patient has virtually no choice as to what doctor he will get. At the hospitals, the patients lie in the corridors, where either the air is stuffy or else there is a draft. There are no "sick-nurses," very few orderlies or practical nurses, and a handful of registered nurses. The situation is bad with regard to linen, medication, and food. For an ordinary hospital, the budget allocates less than one ruble per day per patient for everything.

---

* Discrimination in admissions is effected very simply: Separate categories are created for undesirable high school graduates, and almost no one from these categories is admitted.

Naturally, there is nothing; and conditions are frightful. But for privileged hospitals the budget allocates up to fifteen rubles per day per patient. It is not a matter of accident that all the foreigners I know who are living in Moscow send their wives to capitalist countries for delivery of their babies, even though the care available to them here is incomparably better than that provided for ordinary Soviet citizens.

In the provinces there is almost no modern medication, and even Moscow lags far behind the Western countries in the range of medication available. (Exception: the privileged hospitals and polyclinics for the elites.) There is a prohibition against sending medicines from the West to the USSR by mail. Doctors are forbidden to prescribe scarce or foreign drugs, or even to mention their existence. Thus to deprive a patient of medical help—and even of the knowledge that such help is in principle possible—is a flagrant violation of traditional medical ethics. Undoubtedly, many patients and their relatives would go to any expense, and make any effort, to alleviate suffering or save a life.

Another example of the violation of the principles of medical ethics is a directive from the Ministry of Public Health in accordance with which first priority in medical care must be given to the worker contingent. This directive is addressed, in particular, to rural district doctors.

The system of medical education has been seriously undermined; and in most areas the medical equipment is on a nineteenth-century level. The general ethical and professional decline has spread to the doctors, who held out longer than others. Those unquestionable gains made by medicine in the first decades of the Soviet régime (in pediatrics, in combating infectious diseases, etc.) are now threatened.

Ninth, the low wage level means that a man's earnings do not suffice to support his family, even if he has only one child. Hence the impossibility of a normal family upbringing for children, with serious social consequences. Hence, too, the destruction of the health of millions of women doing heavy work.

Tenth, there is restriction on freedom of movement within the country—the passport system—which for millions of members of collective farms means the impossibility of going off to the city.

The rural population is numerous by Western standards. But the young people are eager to leave the rural areas; and after military service, the men scarcely ever return. There is a large, potentially productive manual labor force (the majority women); but only machinery operators are paid well. Many people simply vegetate. Drunkenness is epidemic everywhere. There is a very sad bit of folklore which goes:

> *What's it like out in the sticks?*
> *Lots of Manyas but few Vanyas.**
> *Lots of vodka but few baths.*
> *And for every ear of grain*
> *The Party hacks†all beat the drums.*

Harsh restrictions on authorized places of residence for former prisoners often wreck their whole lives. The

* That is, lots of women but few men. [Translator]
† *Raikom.* Literally: "regional committee." [Translator]

whole world knows about the immeasurable suffering of the Crimean Tatars, who 31 years ago became the victims of a criminal resettlement during which half of the children and old people died of hunger and cold. Yet even now they are being denied their right to return to their native Crimea, which badly needs their labor. And their fate has been shared by the Volga Germans, the Meskhi Turks, and others.

Eleventh, it is impossible for most citizens to travel abroad—not even on tourist trips, not to mention tours in connection with one's work, or trips for the purpose of earning money, studying, or receiving medical treatment. Compare the following. It is estimated that half of the 32 million persons from the Federal Republic of Germany taking a month's paid vacation in August 1975 will spend their holidays abroad, many accompanied by their families.

Twelfth, the finishing touch to this portrait of a society is "lumpenization": the dissipation and tragic alcoholism of the great mass of the population, including women and young people. The per capita consumption of alcohol is thrice what it was in tsarist Russia. The authorities' attitude toward this frightful calamity among the people is ambivalent. On the one hand, it is too bad that people go on so many sprees, and that in the morning the workers' hands tremble. But on the other hand, the people are more docile this way. They demand less, and the money flows spontaneously back into the government's pocket. And in general, they say, that's the way it's always been in Russia, and it's not up to us to change it. Meantime, in the Russian Republic alone 10,000 drunkards collapse and freeze on the streets every year. And all those cities and towns that have no such army of policemen as Moscow are groaning from the spreading epidemic of senseless, brutal hooliganism and crime.

It is extremely significant that our society lacks social justice. Although the appropriate sociological studies either have not been carried out in our country, or have been classified as secret, it may be affirmed that as early as the 1920's and 30's—and definitively in the postwar years—a special Party-bureaucratic stratum was formed and could be discerned. This is the *nomenklatura*, as its members call themselves; or the "new class," as Milovan Djilas has named them.* This elite has its own life style, its own clearly defined social status—"bosses" and "chiefs"—and its own way of talking and thinking. The *nomenklatura* has in fact an inalienable status, and has recently become hereditary. Thanks to a complex system of covert and overt official privileges, along with contacts, acquaintanceships, and mutual favors—and also thanks to their high salaries—these people are able to live in much better housing,† and to feed and clothe themselves better (often for less money in special

* In Orwell's famous prophetic novel *1984*, this is the "inner party." In East Germany an amusing phrase, *Sie-Gelnossen*—"comrades addressed in the second person plural"—has recently come into use.

† Pursuant to a special government decree, all "ordinary" citizens have been resettled from midtown Moscow. They have been relocated in new suburban areas with standard apartment buildings and provided with individual flats for each family (which are cramped by Western standards but much better

"closed" stores or for currency certificates,* or by means of trips abroad—which, under Soviet conditions, constitute the highest award for loyalty).

Recently a large group of students who had been graduated with honors from various colleges in the country were brought together for a month in Leningrad under some plausible pretext. (Naturally, they were Komsomol members: today college student bodies consist almost exclusively of Komsomol members.) They were lavishly wined and dined at the best restaurants, and entertained in every way—all at no expense to them. In short, they lived off the fat of the land. Then they were asked: "Would you like to live like this the rest of your life? If so, go to the VPSh." (The VPSh

---

than the Moscow communal apartments), and they are very glad about it. Meanwhile, the old private houses and other monuments of Old Moscow are being ruthlessly torn down to make way for the construction of luxury buildings to be occupied by a carefully selected elite. All utilities and services for these buildings must meet the highest standards. Not only that, but a special canal is being constructed to supply particularly pure water. (It is said that this canal is very undesirable from an economic point of view.) Around Moscow there is a ring of special luxury dachas, each surrounded by high, impassable fences. This is the chief bastion of the triumphant *nomenklatura* —the symbol of power and prosperity. The dacha remaining to me from my past is an example.

* In the Soviet Union, these certificates are called "money for the whites," as distinguished from "money for the blacks"—Soviet rubles. (In accordance with the conventional notion, the whites are privileged and the blacks are downtrodden.) The states' currency operations constitute a special and rather ticklish subject. There is good reason why those citizens who infringe these prerogatives are punished and sometimes executed.

is the Higher Party School, upon graduation from which even a minimally gifted person can become at least the second secretary of a regional committee.) History, I should say, tells us a lot. In the 1920's this would have been impossible.

Among the masses of the population there is considerable resentment, both over the privileges of the *nomenklatura,* for which ordinary citizens bear the expense, and over the often obvious blunders of the bureaucratic style of management. Even a person far removed from politics cannot fail to notice such things as the rotting, every year, of a substantial part of the harvest of vegetables, fruit, and grain; the spoilage of almost 50 percent of the mineral fertilizers in transit to the fields; overfishing; the loss of fish from pollution in reservoirs and as a result of violations of spawning conditions; the destruction of forests; the erosion of soils—those great riches of the country; extravagant and predatory hunting expeditions by high officials in game preserves; the flooding of meadows; flagrant blunders in the planning and practice of industrial construction; lack of concern for convenient transportation, water supply, utilities, and in general for the day-to-day life of ordinary citizens; and the harsh and senseless regulation of the employees, and of the financial and economic activity of all institutions.

It often happens, of course, that by virtue of tradition, ignorance, prejudices, and various kinds of conformism, that this resentment is displaced toward the intelligentsia (which itself is an oppressed element), and toward citizens of different ethnic origins. (These include the Jews in Russia, Belorussia, and the Ukraine; the Russians in the republics of Central Asia and the Baltic region; the Armenians in Azerbaijan and Georgia; etc. Even the few "colored" students from the Third World countries are the object of a barbarous race hatred.)* Similarly "displaced" is the widespread dislike of Khrushchev, who despite his many "deviations"† that damaged the country, made a valuable contribution in many areas of life. (I refer to the release of prisoners from the Stalin era, raising the daily wages on the collective farms, increasing pensions; expanding housing construction; seeking new approaches to international relations; attempting to improve the style of leadership; trying to limit the privileges of the *nomenklatura;* and proposing cuts in excessive military expenditures. The last two initiatives were the chief cause of Khrushchev's downfall in 1964.)

In all justice it should be noted that the Brezhnev administration, while ostensibly rather more than cool toward everything associated with the name of Khrushchev, has in fact appropriated a considerable share of the positive initiatives of that era, though it in no way publicizes that continuity and uses great caution. Yet

---

* This "Great Russian" or "Great Soviet" chauvinism is often manifested by Soviet citizens abroad. There is good reason why, in Arab and other countries where there are many resident Soviet specialists, the latter are frequently hated for their contemptuous attitude toward the local inhabitants.

† For example, the severe restrictions on private garden plots; senseless and disastrous management in agriculture and in the arts; intensifying religious persecutions; aggravating poor conditions in places of confinement; etc.

something has been lost. And, most important, in all these years the events have followed the laws of the socialist system, which have yielded but slightly to correctives from either above or below and have brought out with increasing clarity the gap between the foundations of the system and the demands of modern times.

Foreign visitors sometimes ask: Why, if you really have so many shortcomings, don't the people take steps to correct them? There is no simple answer to that question. One of the reasons for the stability of the régime is the fact that living standards are rising, however slowly. Naturally, each person compares his life not with distant and inaccessible Paris or New York but with his own poverty-stricken past. But there is a still more important factor: the immanent strength of the totalitarian régime—the inertia of fear and passivity. No nation has, in one generation, made such incomparable sacrifices. The Soviet worker is not an English (nor even a Polish) longshoreman who can, if need be, simply take a walk. Although the radio daily informs the ordinary Soviet citizen that he is the master of his country, he realizes very well that the real masters are those who, morning and evening, speed through the deserted, closed-off streets in their armored limousines. He has not forgotten how his grandfather was dispossessed as a kulak. And he knows that even today his personal fate depends wholly upon the state: upon his immediate or remote superiors; upon the chairman of the housing committee; upon the chairman of the trade union committee, who may or may not decide to get his child into kindergarten; and possibly on the KGB informer working next to him. When elections come around, he drops his ballot—with one name on it—into the box. He must realize how much he is politically humiliated by such an election without a contest. He cannot fail to understand the insult to common sense and human dignity implicit in this "splendid" ceremony. He is subjected to the same kind of training as a horse; and he submits to the training in order to survive. He deceives himself. The Soviet citizen is a result of a totalitarian society and, for the time being, its chief support. I can only pray that the emergence from this historical dead end will not be accompanied by the kind of gigantic shock waves that we cannot yet imagine. That is why I am an evolutionist—a reformist.

The consequences of the Party-State monopoly are especially destructive in the sphere of culture and ideology. The complete unification of ideology at all times and places—from the school desk to the professorial chair—demands that people become hypocrites, timeservers, mediocre, and stupidly self-deceiving. The tragicomic, ritualistic farce of the loyalty oath is played over and over, relegating to the background all considerations of practicality, common sense, and human dignity. Writers, artists, actors, teachers, and scholars are under such monstrous ideological pressure that one wonders why art and the humanities have not altogether vanished in our country. The influence of those same anti-intellectual factors on the exact sciences and the applied sciences is more indirect but no less destructive. A comparison of scientific, technological, and economic achievements in the USSR and abroad makes this perfectly plain. It is no accident that for many years, in our country, new and promising scientific trends in biology and cybernetics could not develop normally, while on the surface out-and-out demagogy, ignorance, and charlatanism bloomed like gorgeous flowers. It is no accident that all the great scientific and technological discoveries of recent times—quantum mechanics, new elementary particles, uranium fission, antibiotics and most of the new, highly effective drugs, transistors, electronic computers, the development of highly productive strains in agriculture, the discovery of other components of the "Green Revolution," and the creation of new technologies in agriculture, industry, and construction—all of them happened outside our country.

The significant achievements in the first decade of the space age, which were due to the personal qualities of the late Academician S. P. Korolev and to certain fortuitous features of our programs for building military rockets, which made possible their direct use in space—constitute an exception which does not disprove the rule. And certain successes in military technology are the result of an enormous concentration of resources in that sphere.

Ideological monism and intolerance, together with cold (although not wise) political calculation, are causing an unrelenting persecution of dissidents. In the USSR there are anywhere from 2,000 to 10,000 individuals who can be identified as political prisoners. (This figure does not include those suffering for their religious convictions. Apparently there are even more of the latter. I should also qualify this by saying that

31

my information may be incomplete.) According to the Code now in force, all political prisoners are regarded as common criminals. They share with prisoners of other categories (often including innocent persons) the hardships and humiliations of a life the character of which is shameful and unacceptable in our time. Attempts to publicize details about conditions of confinement and the daily life of prisoners bring harsh reprisals—which is the best proof of the fact that there is something to hide. Yet a good deal is known: the heavy forced labor, which often involves violations of safety measures; a diet both insufficient and bad, and the virtual impossibility of improving it via parcels mailed or brought in, since these are severely restricted (the same restraints exist even under conditions of preliminary detention); severe limitations on visits, correspondence, and the opportunity to obtain books; harsh, arbitrary controls. The political prisoners' struggle for their human rights—recently there has been news of many heroic hunger strikes—leads, as a rule, only to new repressions.

The Soviet prison (and camp) system bears many of the characteristics of that even more terrifyingly vast Gulag—described by Solzhenitsyn, Shalamov, Ginzburg, Olitskaya, and hundreds of other eyewitnesses and researchers—which annihilated more than 20 million persons.[*]

---

[*] For those of us who have grown up in this country, the personal impressions, reminiscences, and testimonials of relatives and friends, often no less frightful than what is described in books, carry more weight than the latter.

From time to time, amnesties are declared. (The last two, respectively, were on the fiftieth anniversary of the founding of the USSR and the thirtieth anniversary of the end of the war.) But they have been of a limited, special character, and have not been applied to political prisoners. Moreover, the administration at the place of confinement is authorized to refuse to apply the amnesty to any prisoner, under the pretext that he has violated the regulations.

In order to correct the existing, unacceptable situation, it is essential to establish international monitoring of prisons, labor camps, and special psychiatric hospitals (where conditions are even worse), and to grant a general amnesty to political prisoners.

But who are the Soviet political prisoners? The great majority of them have never perpetrated crimes as the word is understood in democratic countries. They have not committed acts of violence, nor have they incited to them. One of the commonest causes of political repressions is the reading, keeping, or passing on to friends of *samizdat* typescripts and books of undesirable content (although usually they are essentially harmless). A list of the books that have been the occasion of arrests and convictions would include (there is no index of prohibited books; everyone must imagine for himself): Pasternak's *Doctor Zhivago*, Akhmatova's *Requiem*, Berdyaev's *The Sources and Meaning of Russian Communism*, Orwell's *1984*, Grossman's *Forever Flowing*, the present author's *Thoughts on Progress . . .*, Avtorkhanov's *Technology of Power*, Solzhenitsyn's *Gulag Archipelago*, the works of Djilas, Conquest's *The Great*

Terror, *samizdat* journals, such as the *Chronicle of Current Events, Veche* [*Popular Assembly*], the *Chronicle of the Lithuanian Catholic Church,* and a great many others.° In this connection it should be remembered that while in the capital cities the KGB organs have given up the Stalinist practice of preventive removal of potential critics from society, in the provinces this practice is still followed on a limited scale. Many people, usually young, often from the working class or the provincial intelligentsia, whose first timid doubts are combined with disarming illusions about the Soviet régime, go straight to prison or a camp. (Most of the workers, Party members, and people who declare they are Marxists, are sent to the horrible special psychiatric hospitals—obviously out of considerations of "decency.")

The prisons—and especially the psychiatric hospitals—are crowded with people who tried secretly to leave the country (or, with the same end in mind, ran the blockade into foreign embassies), after having despaired of exercising that right through official channels. Many Crimean Tatars and Meskhi Turks are in confinement.†

Among those suffering for their convictions, the religious believers constitute a large group. The perse-

---

° Sergei Pirogov was indicted for having given, to the relatives of a suicide, a note written by the latter which chanced to come into his hands, the content of the note being allegedly libelous. Victor Nekipelov and Petrov-Agatov were indicted for their poetry.

† At the present time Mustafa Dzhemilev, one of the most courageous fighters for the right of the Crimean Tatars to live on their native soil, is threatened with a third sentence.

cution of religion is a frightful tradition in all the socialist countries; but nowhere (except perhaps in Albania) has it attained such scope and depth as in the USSR. In the 1920's and 30's the blows were aimed at the sects with the largest followings—Orthodoxy and Islam—and the victims were countless. Today these religions have been so humiliated, and they are so deprived of rights (at least on the surface), that they have almost become appendages of the state. (By no means do I want to belittle the importance of these faiths or the inner nonconformism of their adherents.)

Today the focus of the repressions has plainly shifted to relatively small religious groups who demonstrate great obstinacy: the Uniates, Baptists, Catholics, followers of the True Orthodox Church, Pentecostalists, and Buddhists. Much is known about the persecutions of these groups, about the economic sanctions, and the trials resulting in long sentences. Recently, special attention has been given the conviction of the Baptists P. V. Rumachik and Georgy P. Vins; the tragic death in a labor camp of Bidiya Dandaron, who had been sentenced for his religious activities; and the brutal murder of a Pentecostalist deacon, who had wanted to emigrate to the United States together with his flock. One of the most inhuman forms of religious persecution is the removal of children from their parents in order to protect them from a "pernicious" religious upbringing. Religious persecution is a flagrant violation of the principle of separation of church and state—the kind of meddling by the state in the personal convictions of citizens that is intolerable in a democratic society.

Many political prisoners are nationalists from the Ukraine, the Baltic republics, and Armenia. Especially severe sentences have been meted out to those people, who in most cases have been prosecuted because of their concern for preserving their national cultures in the face of a threat of Russification. In Armenia, twenty-seven-year-old Paruir Airikyan, who had previously served seven years, was sentenced to a further eight years.

One of the characteristics of trials on political charges is the violation of the principle of a public hearing (quite simply, no one is allowed in the courtroom except for two or three close relatives and some KGB agents), and the fact that there isn't even the semblance of an impartial proceeding. Up to now it has been difficult for the Western observer fully to believe this phenomenon. Like many other situations in our country, it is something that must be seen with one's own eyes.

The so-called slanderous fabrications known to be false—the basic charge in political trials—are never really verified by the court. It suffices that they seem (or should seem) slanderous to the procurator, the judges, and the KGB.

Special note must be taken of the fate of those individuals prosecuted because of their concern for the fate of others who they believe have been unjustly convicted; and because of their attempts to secure justice and public disclosure. Such has been the lot of Leonid Plyushch, a member of the Initiative Group for the defense of human rights in the USSR, who in the Dnepropetrovsk psychiatric hospital was subjected to tortures bordering on psychic murder; or Vladimir

Bukovsky and Semyon Gluzman, each sentenced to seven years of incarceration° for having exposed psychiatric repressions; and of Andrei Tverdokhlebov and Sergei Kovalev, both recently arrested; and many others. It is in fact citizens like these, united by repressions and a resolve to follow the dictates of their hearts and convictions, who form what may be called the "democratic movement." Despite the small number of such people, mostly concentrated in a few of the country's largest cities and not joined together in any organized way, the ethical significance of their very existence in the monolith of Soviet society is immeasurable.

I am convinced that the defense of Soviet political prisoners and other dissenters, the struggle for greater humanity in places of imprisonment and for human rights in general, is not only the moral duty of honest persons throughout the world but constitutes a direct defense of human rights in their own countries. But we often encounter a lack of interest in our misfortunes. After a visit to the Soviet Union by Harold Wilson, the British prime minister (to whom I had sent my usual appeal), I heard on the radio a placid commentary by a journalist who said Wilson could not allow himself to meddle in matters of human rights in the USSR, since those problems were basically of interest to "rightist" elements, and he could not make common cause with them. I hope Wilson's real position was nothing like that. But still, what levels of cynicism are possible!

° Not necessarily "imprisonment." Gluzman is in fact now in a labor camp in Perm. [Translator]

In February of 1975, the German writer Heinrich Böll and I issued a joint appeal (addressed to Brezhnev and Kosygin) for an amnesty of political prisoners and for an improvement in the conditions of detention. We particularly singled out Vladimir Bukovsky, Semyon Gluzman, Leonid Plyushch, and a number of other political captives, including women in a Mordovian labor camp. I hope that this appeal did not go unnoticed abroad and that in our country it became known to those upon whom the restoration of justice depends.

In past decades, millions perished in complete anonymity. The change in this country's situation has made it possible to breach the conspiracy of silence; and many selfless, bold, and talented people have decided—and have been able—to take advantage of that situation. But this is a feat of valor that can involve new sacrifices and new victims. Great services have been rendered by the publishers of the *Chronicle of Current Events,* an anonymous *samizdat* information bulletin, and by certain other groups and individuals acting alone. A role has been played by those writers who have managed to expose to the world carefully concealed aspects of our society. I refer not only to the labor camps but to the whole psychological, social, moral, and economic situation. In exposing the crimes of the camps, many eyewitnesses have been resentenced for their truthful testimony. I am thinking in particular of three extraordinary men whose fate has been alarming: Anatoly Marchenko, Danylo Shumuk, and Yury Shukhevich. Victor Khaustov and Gabriel Superfin have been sentenced to long terms of imprisonment. According to the courts, they had some connection with the publication abroad of Eduard Kuznetsov's *Prison Diaries.** He was one of those convicted in the Leningrad "airplane case" of attempting to leave the country.

For many years the KGB has been especially vehement in persecuting those having any connection with the *Chronicle of Current Events,* with its distribution, or (presumably) with its publication. And the complaisant courts have, without evidence, declared the *Chronicle* to be "libelous," and meted out sentences generously.

One judicial investigator recently stated that the *Chronicle* is a libelous publication if 10 percent of its information is false. But no one has yet cited examples of mistakes amounting to even 1 percent—although errors are of course possible in principle, and the anonymous editors have shown their willingness to correct any such. Among those individuals in whose indictments circulation of the *Chronicle* was the chief charge, I want especially to mention two scientists convicted in 1972: Kronid Lyubarsky, the well-known astrophysicist, and Alexander Bolonkin, the mathematician.

Over the years there have been those who repented of their allegedly wrong acts; but on the whole the history of the *Chronicle* is the history of a total moral defeat of the organs of power. In May of 1974, three persons—Sergei Kovalev, Tatyana Khodorovich, and Tatyana Velikanova—announced that they would assume responsibility for circulating the *Chronicle.* The signifi-

---

* Published in the West in 1975. [Translator]

cance of that bold act has been confirmed by the recent arrest of one of the three, the gifted biologist Kovalev.

Sergei Kovalev is a member of the Soviet branch of Amnesty International, an international organization with the mission of defending, everywhere in the world, political prisoners ("prisoners of conscience," as they are called by that organization) who have not committed acts of violence or incited to them. This organization is highly respected for its political impartiality, humanity, and social-consciousness. This makes the arrest of one of its Soviet members even more regrettable. But the story doesn't end there. On April 18, 1975, the secretary of the Soviet chapter of Amnesty International, Andrei Tverdokhlebov, was arrested in Moscow. Tverdokhlebov is well known as a man of irreproachable principles, with an exceptional mind and spiritual qualities, who has accomplished a great deal in the defense of human rights. On that same day, searches were carried out at the homes of Valentin Turchin, chairman of the Soviet branch of Amnesty International, and Vladimir Albrekht, a member of the group; another member, the Ukrainian writer Mikola Rudenko, was detained after further search. On May 27, Rudenko was expelled from the Writers' Union of the Ukraine. (He was expelled *in absentia*; that is, in violation of the charter. And at the session it was noted that he belonged to a "bourgeois organization.") These instances of persecuting Amnesty International members have already provoked protests throughout the world. Such persecutions are of course completely inadmissible in a democratic country.

I hope that Amnesty International will send representatives to the trials of its members. The Soviet authorities would bring great shame upon themselves if they refused to let Amnesty International do this.

Also very significant, along with judicial persecutions, are extrajudicial persecutions: dismissals from jobs, trying to prevent one's children from acquiring an education or a job, etc. I believe people in the West have a limited understanding of the seriousness of these conditions in our totalitarian state. I find meaningful the fates of two outstanding scientists—Doctor of Sciences Valentin Turchin, a physicist and mathematician, and Associate Member of the Armenian Academy of Sciences Yury Orlov, a physicist, who more than a year ago were dismissed from their posts for publicly speaking out in my defense in September 1973.

The statements issued by both men were quiet in tone and displayed no disloyalty to the state—in complete accordance with the authors' tolerant and benevolent states of mind—and they contained thoughts that were not harmful. But upon a signal from the KGB their frightened superiors and colleagues "took steps." Orlov and Turchin, after this kind of ideological dismissal, cannot find any other work. They are deprived of all means of subsistence. It is even difficult for them to scrape up private students. Individuals who find themselves in this kind of situation are lucky if they can earn 100 rubles ($50) for ten days work as a helper at a construction project.

Other forms of extrajudicial persecution include: deportation (applied to Alexander Solzhenitsyn); creating conditions so that a person is obliged to emigrate, which is factually equivalent to deportation (There are many examples of this. The most recent, and most tragic, is the case of Anatoly Marchenko. After Marchenko had refused, for reasons of principle, to emigrate via Israel— something his oppressors wanted—he was arrested and sentenced to internal exile); depriving persons who are traveling abroad of Soviet citizenship (Valery Chalidze and Zhores Medvedev). My friend Chalidze was the first such victim. At the time, yielding to emotions and unfounded apprehensions, I published an equivocal statement on the incident. There are few actions I regret so much.

There is great tragedy in the fate of those citizens who were sentenced to twenty-five years of imprisonment prior to 1958, when new legislation set the maximum sentence at fifteen years. Usually, any law alleviating the lot of convicted persons has retroactive force. But by a special resolution of the USSR Supreme Soviet (not one of the deputies showed any scruples about it), these prisoners are still in labor camps. One of them, the Lithuanian writer Peter Paulaitis, was assigned by the Nazis to a death camp in 1943 for having saved a group of Jews, but he escaped. In 1946 he was sentenced to twenty-five years for publishing an underground nationalist newspaper. In 1956 he was amnestied. Two months later, without new grounds, he was again sentenced to twenty-five years. He now resides in a Mordovian camp for political prisoners. Another Lithuanian, Ludvigas Simutis, greatly respected by his friends for his honesty and principles, is serving a term of twenty-five years (up to 1980). He has tuberculosis of the bone, and only occasionally is able to leave his hospital bed. The stories of the Ukrainians Evgeny Pronyuk and Svyatoslav Karavansky,* and dozens of others, are no less dramatic.

Although I have never laid eyes on any of these people, I cannot fail to be shaken by their experiences, which call to mind stories of prisoners in medieval dungeons. Or, in our day, the fate of Rudolf Hess. I mention Hess, even though I am aware of his participation in creating the criminal Nazi system, but I consider life imprisonment to be the equivalent of capital punishment. I oppose capital punishment as a matter of principle, regardless of the nature of the crime.

For several centuries thinkers from many countries—including Beccaria, Hugo, and Tolstoi—have consistently called for the abolition of capital punishment as an immoral, inhumane, and harmful institution. In recent years capital punishment has ceased in the majority of the developed countries. But in the USSR this step is considered "premature." And every year, from 700 to 1,000 persons (according to my own rough estimate) are shot, on a wide variety of charges ranging from homicide with aggravating circumstances to the "theft of state property on an especially large scale," prohibited currency operations, and other charges unfamiliar in Western law. None of these cases is reported in the press, and usually they are known only to a

* Karavansky has been in prison almost continually since 1944. His most recent sentence was for gathering information on the Katyn Forest massacre.

limited circle. Moreover, the overall picture of crime—and statistics in particular—is generally kept closely secret. It is also significant that the juristic and moral level of court proceedings in the country is beneath criticism.*

In my country, many grave crimes are committed—often owing to drunkenness and other social causes. I realize that these misfortunes happen everywhere in the world, although with varying degrees of seriousness. I am convinced that they can be alleviated, not by a continuation and intensification of repressions, but only through a moral upsurge, through people's turning to simple and true values shared by all mankind, through bringing the people of the world closer together, through the things that make people happier and give them more spiritual freedom. The abolition of capital punishment is essential to our country, poisoned by a spirit of brutality and indifference to human suffering.

In concluding this chapter, I want to touch upon a few individual matters. Recently a discussion was provoked in *samizdat* and the foreign press by some stinging statements from Alexander Solzhenitsyn and Igor Shafarevich on basic questions of the present and future of our country. Some of Solzhenitsyn's theses struck

---

* In the 1960's, during a routine campaign against corruption, the majority of the procurators and judges in one of the *raions* of Moscow were removed for systematically taking bribes. The principle of the presumption of innocence is officially recognized. But this is meaningless not only to the people's assessors [That is, the two laymen who, together with the judge, constitute a court of first instance in the Soviet Union. (Translator)] but to the judges sitting on criminal cases.

me as untrue and disturbing, and I considered it necessary to say as much in a brief statement that I published. Later Solzhenitsyn amplified his views and defined them more precisely. Today I see no reason for continuing the debate. But while not arguing with anyone in particular, I should nonetheless like to formulate my own viewpoint.

The salvation of our country—in its interdependence with all the rest of the world—is impossible without saving all of humanity. The appeal for national repentance on the part of Russia—an appeal born out of long suffering—is noble. It is set in opposition to Great Russian expansion—against national guilt and calamities. But are not both these matters due to one and the same fateful philosophical error—an error that inevitably entails moral harm and tragic consequences? For it is not a matter of accident that religion and life-affirming systems of ethical philosophy (for example, the views of Albert Schweitzer) put their emphasis on the human being and not on the nation. It is specifically the human being who is called upon to acknowledge guilt and succor his neighbor.

We must have democratic reforms affecting all aspects of life. The future of the Soviet Union lies in an orientation toward progress, science, and a personal and social moral regeneration. The modalities of that regeneration must not be limited to religious or nationalist ideologies, or to patriarchal aspirations in the spirit of Rousseau. No one should count on the rapid and universal solution of great problems. We must all endow ourselves with patience and tolerance—combining them, however, with boldness and consistency of thought. But we must not call upon our people, our youth, to make sacrifices. The people of the Soviet Union are totally dependent upon the state. It can swallow each of them without choking. And we have already had more than enough of sacrifices and victims.

The chief difficulties with carrying out a far-reaching reform without a complete spectrum of democratic political and social transformations are illustrated in one tragic episode. A man by the name of Khudenko, who headed up a "socio-economic" experiment authorized under Khrushchev, died in prison about a year ago. As the head of a big state farm, he was given complete autonomy in all financial, economic, and personnel matters. He succeeded in reducing fivefold the number of workers on the state farm, while at the same time increasing output. Production costs were cut, but the wages of workers were raised several times. It was plain that these changes were advantageous to the workers and the nation; but they ran counter to the conservatism, cowardice, and selfish interests of the *nomenklatura*. So they decided to get rid of Khudenko. When the state farm was closed down by order of a republic ministry, Khudenko filed a petition in court demanding that the workers be paid the money they had earned. He was charged with attempting to damage the state on an especially large scale. The punishment for this kind of crime ranges up to the death penalty. But he was accorded "clemency" (in view of his past services, his family situation, and the state of his health), and was sentenced to eight years of incarceration—which nonetheless turned out to be a death sentence for him.

The internal specifics of the system have weighty consequences in matters of foreign policy—something I shall discuss in succeeding chapters. For the moment I want to emphasize only certain facts: first of all, the secretiveness of our society, and the totalitarian, privy° character of the administration, which can make decisions in secret, without any prior open discussion, and the huge, unaudited financial resources for covert operations in other countries. It is likewise significant that all of our country's relations with the rest of the world, both covert and overt—diplomatic, commercial, scientific, propagandistic—can be purposefully controlled in accordance with a single plan, a single will. All these specifics endow Soviet foreign policy with special traits: great dynamism and a pragmatic lack of principle. The latter is manifested, for example, in the support—by means of huge shipments of Soviet weapons—of the tyrannical regimes of Amin in Uganda, el-Qaddafi in Libya, and many other such countries. Also, our government has supported the genocide of the Ibo people in Nigeria, the Kurds in Iraq, etc., and exploited national, religious, and political enmities in many parts of the world for purposes of expansionism.

These characteristics make it possible to violate agreements with impunity. They encourage cruelty. And they open up tremendous possibilities for covert subversive operations in other countries: bribery, deceit,

° *Kabinetni*—"behind closed doors." [Translator]

blackmail, and the organization of "fifth columns." And there is an additional danger—an additional challenge—to mankind, which already finds itself in an extremely complex situation. It is the supermilitarism of the USSR that necessitates high military expenditures throughout the world.

The chronic malaise of agriculture in our country—which before the Revolution was the breadbasket of Europe—is one of the chief factors complicating the solution of the world food problem.

The socialist countries' lack of economic levers for regulating the economy; their bureaucratic pseudo-planning; their secretiveness; the irresponsibility of their bureaucracy—all these matters make it difficult to cooperate with the socialist countries in preserving the environment.

A broad public awareness of these facts and their interrelationships is extremely important. Only under such conditions can coordinated, purposeful actions to counter the dangers threatening humanity be carried out.

As it happens, this chapter has turned out to be, by Soviet standards, rather "malignant." From time to time, in those agonizing hours after working, I have experienced a feeling of embarrassment—almost of shame. Am I really doing something that matters? I think of all those who are performing their useful jobs: growing wheat and sugar beets; building houses, bridges, and automobiles; treating children or filling teeth; writing poetry or working in laboratories—and believing that they are helpful to people; and dreaming of personal happiness. But I am not betraying any of them; I am not casting aspersions on their honest labor and their dreams. Nor am I betraying myself or my own potential. (Such betrayal is, after all, a bad business.) I may well lack the talent for an essay like this: the acuteness of mind and ability to summarize, the gift of observation, and the knowledge of life demanded by the task that fate has set for me. But if I am inwardly honest, I have nothing to reproach myself for; and I hope my work should prove useful, like any other toiler's.

II

The Freedom to Choose One's Country of Residence

In recent years, public opinion has been focused on the problem of emigration from the USSR, which is part of the more general and very important problems of the freedom to choose one's own country of residence, and one's place of residence and employment within a given country. These rights were proclaimed by the Universal Declaration of Human Rights (Article 13), and confirmed by the Covenants on Rights adopted by the UN General Assembly in 1968. The Government of the USSR ratified the Covenants in 1973, ahead of the other great powers. But the practical implementation of many of these rights in the USSR and the lack of appropriate guarantees in domestic legislation, have aroused serious apprehensions.

During 1974 and 1975 major events took place in this regard. In December 1974 the US Congress passed a trade bill with an amendment which made the granting of credits and most-favored-nation status to the USSR and other socialist countries contingent upon the fulfillment of certain guarantees relating to the right to emigrate. Congress had previously been informed by Secretary of State Kissinger that the Soviet Government had given such guarantees on a private, diplomatic level. Shortly before the bill was passed by Congress, the Soviet Government, in a published note, repudiated the information given by Kissinger; and after the bill was passed, the government unilaterally denounced the 1972 trade agreement, including payments on Lend-Lease. Soon several capitalist countries (Britain, France, Iran, Japan) concluded agreements with the USSR as a result of which the latter obtained credits of $8 billion (according to a statement by President Ford) —an amount far higher than the credit of $350 million offered by the United States.

In the wake of these events the authors of the amendment, along with its other supporters, were subjected to unusually sharp (and, in my view, unjust) criticism.

Those American businessmen who were counting on reaping huge profits from trade with the USSR (chiefly, let it be noted, at the expense of the American taxpayer) were disillusioned with this turn of events, when the business largely passed from their hands into those of their European and Japanese competitors. Politicians who were among the enemies and rivals of Senator Henry Jackson and his adherents also found it feasible to exploit the situation so as to discredit the authors of the amendment. In several articles and speeches, Jackson and his supporters were charged with adventurism and with damaging American economic interests, the policy of détente, and emigration from the USSR. The argument ran as follows. The USSR, as a great sovereign state, could not agree to interference in its internal affairs, so that Jackson's "economic blackmail" had led to a result the opposite of that intended. Unfortunately, President Ford joined the critics. He said in a speech that although Congress, in his opinion, had been guided by humanitarian aims, the amendment that had been passed was counter-productive, since (so he claimed) it complicated the problem of emigration and harmed American economic interests. He also said that methods of "secret diplomacy" were more effective, having brought about an increase in emigration, but that through the fault of the Congress emigration had decreased again.

Many Americans supported the amendment. So far as I know, most members of Congress have assumed a firm and principled position, and are not yielding to Soviet pressure. I was pleased to hear a summary of a speech by the trade-union leader George Meany, who speaks for much of the American working class—a viewpoint with greater perspective than that of many businessmen and politicians I have heard about.

I expressed my own views on the problem in several documents: in an "Open Letter to the Members of the USSR Supreme Soviet" (September 1971); in four appeals to the US Congress from 1973–75; and in a statement written for the Assembly of the National Conference on Soviet Jewry in May 1975. In my statements I supported the arguments of Senator Jackson, and I set forth a few additional considerations.

I feel that the US Congress, in passing the amendment to the trade bill, performed an act of historic significance that continues the best democratic and humanitarian traditions of the American people. I reject the claim advanced by the critics of the amendment that it constitutes intervention in the internal affairs of the USSR. The right to the free choice of one's country of residence is confirmed in the covenants on human rights ratified by the USSR. This right is of prime importance for the purposes of assuring international trust and the openness of Soviet society, which is essential to the security of all mankind. This right is also of great importance to all citizens—both those who are leaving and, especially, those who are remaining behind—as a guarantee of other social and civil rights' being recognized, but only if there is domestic legislation protecting each person desirous of escaping bureaucratic tyranny. I especially stress the humanitarian aspect of the matter. Thousands of persons who want to join their families, or who are anxious to avoid ethnic or other discrimination, or who are subjected to ethnic humiliation, or who are persecuted by the authorities, or who find it impossible, for one reason or another, to live and work in the USSR, and who for whatever other reason have reached the difficult but irreversible decision to leave— all such people must have that right. I also repeat that the *right* to leave must extend to all persons, including those (constituting the great majority) who have no intention of leaving. Only by having *all* his rights is a person free. When you are living in a house with a locked door you feel that you are a prisoner, even if you have no need to go outside and are not beating your head against the door day and night. Today all Soviet citizens are prisoners in that sense.

The passing of the amendment did not in fact undermine emigration. On the contrary, only unremitting pressure on Soviet authorities has made possible those partial successes achieved in recent years—in the case of Jewish emigration, at any rate. But the emigration of other groups is lagging behind. As I write there is a slight temporary decrease in Jewish emigration. (The chief cause of this is that the majority of the most determined people have managed to leave; but there are other, temporary reasons.) Of course this decrease is in no way related to the amendment to the trade bill (it began much earlier)—all the more reason why it cannot serve as an argument against the latter. An analysis of the events surrounding the amendment shows that the real cause of the difficulties was not interference in the internal affairs of the USSR (after all, there is no doubt but that the assurances mentioned by Kissinger were actually given) but rather the lack of unity among the Western countries. The parliaments of the other Western nations did not support the American initiative. It is not merely that London, Bonn, Paris (and Tokyo) passed no legislation similar to the American amendment: there was not even a hint of their discussing the problem. The "credits bait" was provided by counterproposals from other Western countries. This lack of a common front, of a feeling of solidarity, of coordination, was what made the Soviet counter-maneuver possible. But Europeans who have lived through the horrors of Hitlerian fascism should understand the necessity for defending human rights at least as well as Americans. Therefore I trust that in the future that defense will not only be a leitmotiv of the European security conference but will be manifested in various kinds of legislation.

I am convinced that in this basic matter of such great international, humanitarian, and ethical significance, any retreat by the Congress is completely unacceptable. I hope that all international humanitarian organizations (and not just Jewish organizations) will work toward a more far-seeing and more unified policy. The question of the freedom to choose one's country of residence has become a touchstone for the entire process of détente. To some extent it is being decided right now whether détente is to be a comprehensive, in-depth process of historic significance involving the democratization of Soviet society and making it more open, or whether it is to be a cynical political game serving some persons' local and temporary political and economic interests, while in reality constituting a plot behind the backs of peoples, and capitulation to Soviet pressure and blackmail.

I am taking advantage of this opportunity to make an observation that is important above and beyond the question at hand. Despite inflation, the fuel crisis, and difficulties with employment, the economies of the United States and the other developed countries of the West have much healthier foundations than does the chronically strained, militarized, and chaotically managed economy of the USSR. Therefore, if the West can bring itself to make some small, temporary sacrifices, no economic pressure on it will be effective. On the other hand, it will acquire levers for achieving important goals of far-reaching significance.

I should like to conclude this chapter with one more observation. In many newspaper articles, in some radio broadcasts (in particular by the Voice of America), and even in certain speeches made by responsible statesmen, it has been suggested that the more particular question of Jewish emigration to Israel be substituted for the general question of the freedom to choose one's country of residence. I feel that such a substitution would be not only a mistake but extremely harmful. In no way do I want to slight the importance of Jewish emigration to Israel, or its difficulties. I regard it as a phenomenon that has meaning for all mankind and is of basic importance in the tragic thousands-of-years history of the Jewish people. I understand and respect the nationalist sentiments of those Jews who are going off to build and defend their newly acquired homeland, which has come into being after centuries of Diaspora. I know that a great many Jews have relatives abroad. I know that such circumstances as ethnic humiliation—sometimes covert, sometimes overt, and at other times amounting to factual discrimination—together with poor job prospects, very often compel people of Jewish origin to make the decision to leave. I know about the hundreds of would-be Jewish émigrés who for years have tried in vain to get permission to leave; of the repressions and persecutions—which recently have been stepped up again.* But to reduce this whole problem to one of Jewish emigration is a mistake. Such a concentration would emasculate the social and international significance of the right freely to leave one's country and to return. It would mean that for people of other ethnic origins the right to emigrate was left undefended; and it would make possible the taking of reprisals. Finally, such exclusivity would enable Soviet authorities to support traditional anti-Semitism and utilize it, in particular, against the democratic movement.

I want especially to mention the problem for persons of German origin of emigrating to West Germany. For Soviet Germans, ethnic humiliation has become a common experience. Virtually every family has lost one or more members who perished during resettlement, on reservations, or in labor camps. Almost no Soviet German has a higher education. It is impossible for them to maintain their national culture, and even their language is half-forgotten. At school or at work they constantly hear the epithet "fascists"—the fruit of a nationalistic and militarized culture, showing the influence of radio, television, and, unhappily, the schools. Up to now emigration by Soviet Germans to West Germany has re-

* The recent sentencing of two Jews—Mark Nashpits and Boris Tsitlenok—to five years of internal exile for having taken part in a demonstration is another confirmation of this alarming tendency. Also, in the conviction, in Vinnitsa, of Honored Dr. Mikhail Shtern, I see an attitude of contempt for the medical profession that would be unthinkable, it seems to me, in any other country. And there are reports that new repressions are in the making.

ceived little support from abroad. Much of the blame for this must be borne by the social organizations and political leaders of West Germany. The Germans are particularly vulnerable to the authorities' demand, when an application for a visa is submitted, that an invitation from near relatives to go abroad must be produced (often, through the arbitrary interpretations of the authorities, this would mean parents who were long ago buried in the steppes of Kazakhstan), plus a reference from their place of employment. Thousands of Germans are formally refused each year, and their lives are unsettled. Many have been incarcerated because they wanted to emigrate. Some of my foreign friends say that many Germans who manage to go to West Germany find it hard to adapt to the new life—that they become a burden there. But the fact remains that for all those here who have decided to leave, life is impossible—they are simply perishing.

I am very grateful to Senator James Buckley for his understanding attitude toward this problem and his acceptance of a list of 6,000 Germans from Kazakhstan who want to be repatriated to West Germany. This list is by no means exhaustive. It was compiled by a group of selfless people (some of them are now imprisoned for it), and was transmitted to me by a Soviet German, Friedrich Ruppel, who recently emigrated to West Germany. Senator Buckley passed the list on to Chancellor Helmut Schmidt; and I hope there will be improvements in the hard lot of those persons named on the list.

The situation with regard to emigration is also tragic

for many other groups: the Armenians (including those who returned to the USSR and now want to leave again), Ukrainians, Russians, Lithuanians, Latvians, Estonians, and representatives of persecuted religious groups, including the Pentecostalists, the Baptists, and others. One special group is composed of people who want to emigrate (or simply go) to socialist countries, usually for family reasons. Given the dependence of these countries on the USSR, the position of such people is hopeless. All of these people need international protection.

A delegation from the US Senate was in Moscow from June 29 to July 2, 1975. According to foreign radio reports, the group held talks aimed at finding a compromise on the amendment to the trade bill. Further, according to unverified information that reached me, some of the senators proposed the following agreement by way of a compromise: The Soviet leaders would promise substantially to facilitate emigration and to raise the quota; Congress would drop the amendment to the trade bill; and then the USSR would renew the trade agreements. If this is true, these senators have proposed capitulation. Surely it is clear that an agreement not backed by a legislative assurance of the right to emigrate could be violated. And even before emigration everyone who wanted to leave would face unlimited tyranny. In other areas of détente it would be quite impossible, after such a shameful capitulation, to counter Soviet blackmail. The long-term consequences could be terrifying. It is also obvious that the proposed agreement would amount to a deal betraying the hopes and possibilities for emigration of the Germans and other non-Jewish people. (As I write I have learned of new arrests among the Germans in preparation for Willy Brandt's visit.)

And why is all this being done? For the sake of expanding trade with the USSR? But what can it give the American and other Western economies except Russian vodka and other such unnecessary items? Some mention gold, raw materials, crude oil, and natural gas. But gold is not a commodity. And if large quantities of gold from Kolyma were dumped on the world market in exchange for real, "live" commodities, it would only increase inflation while giving the working people nothing. As for raw material and fuel, it is scarcely likely that the United States would welcome a repetition, on a larger scale, of the Arab oil blackmail of 1973. America and other democracies should not be so dependent upon the totalitarian countries. There is also a strategic danger inherent in such dependence.

We are left with only the humanitarian and social goal of détente: to democratize the socialist societies, to make them more open to the free exchange of people and information, and hence less dangerous to humankind. But such a goal is not achieved by capitulating to blackmail. I hope that the majority of the US Congress understands this.

III

Problems of Disarmament

The unchecked growth of thermonuclear arsenals and the build-up toward confrontation threaten mankind with the death of civilization and physical annihilation. The elimination of that threat takes unquestionable priority over all other problems in international relations. (I have said this in print many times, and I must repeat it.) This is why disarmament talks, which offer a ray of hope in the dark world of suicidal nuclear madness, are so important. But it seems to me that in this critical problem there exist the same shortcomings as in the approach to détente that I have already discussed: the disunity of the West, the illusions of some people, and the political games being played by others. It is especially important to emphasize that the problems of disarmament cannot be separated from the other basic aspects of détente: overcoming the secretiveness of

Soviet society, strengthening international trust, and weakening the totalitarian character of our country. Even if we are striving to solve only the disarmament problem, its solution nonetheless demands unflagging attention to human problems: to the defense of human rights, and to facilitating exchanges of people and information as the basis for international trust. This "indivisibility of détente" must not be forgotten. The Nixon-Brezhnev and Ford-Brezhnev agreements limiting antimissile defense and offensive strategic weapons are very important. But, speaking as an "outsider,"* I shall stress those features of the agreements that strike me as incomplete and even dangerous.

In general, these features include inadequate attention to problems of verification, misconstruing the peculiarities of our totalitarian state, and underestimating the idiosyncrasies of its strategic doctrine and secretiveness.

In all the disarmament talks, the Soviet side has rigidly resisted verification. There are many reasons for this: the secretiveness of Soviet society; the traditional, and today senseless, spy-mania; the wish to bluff (that is, to give the impression of greater strength that one actually has); the desire to gain the advantage of surprise. Making use of its real strength, good will, and determination, the West must oppose this rigid and unreasonable position with great firmness.

An equally basic problem is the danger that the strategic doctrine and practices of a totalitarian state

* English word in original text. [Translator]

may prove more ruthless toward the population of its own country and toward all mankind, more adventuristic, and more subject to accidents governed by personal factors and decisions secretly taken, than is the case in a democratic state.

Before discussing the agreements in detail, I would like to dwell upon the widespread misconception that for economic reasons the Soviet side has a greater interest in real disarmament than do its Western partners. On the basis of this assumption, far-reaching and, in my opinion, dangerous conclusions have been drawn as to the desirability of unilateral disarmament by the West. Unfortunately, the situation is much more complex. Of course the economic system of our country, tremendously burdened with military expenditures, is under extreme tension; and it is very much in the interests of the majority of the population to reallocate millions of rubles to peaceful purposes. But any basic shift in the militarization of our country's economy is impossible without general political changes. Today the dominant characteristic of the policy of the authorities is not to change anything basic, so as not to destroy the existing equilibrium and, in the final analysis, so as not to jeopardize the elite's status and privileges, which are closely bound up with this equilibrium.* One may well be apprehensive that unilateral disarmament by the West would not encounter a reciprocal response,

* I have already mentioned that among the chief causes of Khrushchev's downfall were his attempt to reduce inordinate military expenditures and his infringement on the privileges of the *nomenklatura*.

and this would create a dangerous disturbance of the existing nuclear balance.

I am convinced that any agreements that would have a real, and not merely symbolic, significance, must include:

One. As a first stage, before a total ban on offensive thermonuclear missiles, a sufficiently low limit (with parity in terms of the overall capacity of the warheads) on the delivery systems of strategic thermonuclear warheads. This formulation presupposes that the maximum overall capacity of warheads deployed on strategic delivery systems be fixed at the same level for the USSR and the United States. Also—and most important—that the limit be sufficiently low so that even if all the warheads hit the enemy's cities, only a fraction of the buildings would be destroyed, and only a small part of the population would be killed.

Two. Banning the deployment and improvement of strategic antimissile defense systems. A total ban on MIRVs.* These requirements strike me as realistic, since the realization of these weapons systems is in its initial stage. Refraining from full realization of these systems is important both by virtue of their great cost (at one time it was reported that an ABM [antiballistic missile] system cost four times more than an offensive system of equal capacity) and because their deployment could contribute to strategic instability: Both

* Multiple independently targetable re-entry vehicles. [Translator]

sides might be tempted to make the first strike in order to obtain a decisive advantage.*

Three. A better system of verification, including on-site inspection. The eventual goal of these agreements should be a complete ban on thermonuclear and atomic weapons.

Unfortunately, the agreements that have been reached do not correspond to these ideals. Indeed, one gets the impression that in certain respects they point in the other direction.

In particular, objections and apprehensions have been provoked by the Nixon-Brezhnev agreement on ABM systems. This agreement grants both the USSR and the United States the right to defend one region (in the case of the USSR, the Moscow region) with a small number of ABMs. According to some estimates, the number of installations required for effective defense is much greater (perhaps thirty times greater) than that specified in the agreement. Therefore, in the absence of on-

---

* The relationship between "strategic instability" and the development of MIRVs is discussed in detail *infra*. As regards antimissile defense, see also several studies and articles published abroad in 1966–68 (and my article, "Thoughts . . ."), which discuss the hypothetical case of a sudden thermonuclear-missile attack by a side whose offensive system was equal in capacity to that of the enemy, and who had been the *first* to develop a more effective antimissile defense system. That side could count on decisively damaging his enemy, and avoiding an effective retaliatory strike. The complexity and danger associated with antimissile defenses are increased by the defective nature of the verification system.

the-spot verification, it is possible that one side could secretly increase the number of its installations.

Furthermore, Soviet citizens know that the Moscow region is not only the military-industrial heart of the nation but by and large the elite's enclave. Involuntarily, one entertains a horrible, lurking suspicion and envisions a state of affairs in which, with such a defense system, a great part of the country's territory and population is being sacrificed to the temptation to gain a decisive first-strike advantage with relative security for the Moscow officials.

Only further agreements can clarify this situation. I hope that such agreements will be reached in the shortest possible time.

No less alarming are certain aspects of the agreements on offensive thermonuclear missiles. Here again, there are shortcomings in the verification. Whereas surface and underground launch sites can still be more or less detected by reconnaissance satellites, all other methods of deploying missiles (using underwater and mobile launching platforms) leave unverified the launching weight of the missiles, the capacity of the warheads, and the proportion of missiles that are MIRVed. The ceiling for the number of delivery systems has been set extraordinarily high. Even a small fraction of the maximum number allowed would be enough to do terrible damage.

Since so much has been written on the effects of nuclear weapons, I shall mention only a few indicative figures.

The explosion of one million tons (one megaton) of TNT—the capacity, for example, of a single light thermonuclear warhead of a Polaris missile—would destroy urban buildings over an area of about 50 square kilometers and burn everything in that area that is flammable. Even if shelters were available, hundreds of thousands of people would be killed. An explosion at ground level or at a relatively low altitude is accompanied by a fallout of radioactive particles in a "radioactive trail" that drifts with the wind. The particles consist of sand and dust sucked up by the blast from the earth's surface and impregnated by the radioactive products of the uranium fission. The cloud from a one-megaton explosion yields a lethal dosage of radiation (from 600 to 1,000 roentgens, and even more in the center) over an area of several thousand square kilometers; the effect of the gamma rays emitted in such a case (the rays that did so much damage at Hiroshima and Nagasaki) is secondary, since these rays are absorbed by the air at a range much shorter than the radius of the shock wave.

According to the Vladivostok agreement, both the USSR and the United States may maintain up to 2,400 carriers of warheads. The agreement said nothing about the capacity of the warheads on one delivery system.

According to data from the literature, the capacities of modern thermonuclear warheads range from 1 megaton (small missiles of the Polaris and similar types) up to 30 megatons and above (bombs and the heaviest missiles). In 1961 the Soviet Union tested a thermonuclear warhead which, in its fully jacketed* combat ("dirty") version, has a capacity of 100 megatons. (Khrushchev reported this at the 22nd Party Congress.)

In an attack, presumably, some of the incoming missiles will be used to neutralize enemy launch sites; and let us assume further that a high percentage of those remaining are knocked down by the other side's ABM system, so that the enemy's cities are reached by, say, only 5 percent of the existing (that is, allowed by the agreement) missile force. This 5 percent will still comprise 120 missiles with thermonuclear warheads whose total destructive capacity I would estimate at 600 megatons. Even on such "modest" assumptions, then, thermonuclear war would inevitably entail the destruction of a great part of the cities, and a major portion of the population, of both of the countries involved.

So far I have considered only those warheads that would have reached their targets. But with the explosion of a great number of warheads, or of individual warheads of substantial capacity, the effect of global radioactive contamination (i.e., contamination that affects the entire earth) takes on special significance. Since the winds can carry radioactive products to all points of the earth, the site of the explosion is completely unimportant as regards the global effect. Explosions that released 200,000 to 500,000 megatons would result in the complete annihilation of every living thing on the earth. Even that fatal extreme is not too

* The reference is to the jacket (envelope) of uranium used in "dirty" bombs. A jacket of lead was used in the test in question, which therefore yielded a lower megatonnage. [Translator]

far beyond the established ceiling. If the total number of Soviet and American warheads reaches the allowed figure of 4,800, with an average capacity of 10 megatons, the capacity will amount to 48,000 megatons. (And this projection does not include Britain, China, and France.)

The complexity of the situation is increased by what we know from published materials about the difference between the launching weights of Soviet and American missiles. In the spring of 1975 United States Secretary of Defense James Schlesinger stated that a Soviet missile can be MIRVed with eight warheads, as against three American warheads, because of the threefold difference in throw weights.

I expect that if future talks do not lead to an agreement limiting the overall capacity of the warheads—with a ceiling sufficiently low—in the near future the United States will equip its missile force with heavier boosters. Then the USSR will take reciprocal measures, and the arms race will only be intensified.

The fact that the Vladivostok agreement seemed to legitimize multiple, independently targetable warheads is also alarming. It has been noted many times that this new fashion in military rocketry opens up new possibilities for the arms race and increases the danger of a so-called unstable strategic situation. Put quite simply, it would become strategically advantageous, and relatively safe, for either side to deliver a preemptive strike with nuclear missiles. (That is, in the language of human beings, to commit the greatest crime in history.)

Western authors explain the problem in the following

terms. Let us assume that each of the potential belligerents maintains about the same number of missiles, with roughly the same payload capacities; and that half the missiles of each belligerent are MIRVed with from four to six warheads. Let us further assume that it requires an average of two warheads to knock out one launch site. It is plain that the belligerent who unexpectedly delivers the first strike will be able, with 70 to 100 percent of his MIRVed missiles, to immediately destroy all of the enemy's launch sites, while with his remaining, "conventional" missiles he can destroy all of the enemy's cities plus his military-industrial and transport facilities and thus deal him a crushing blow, doing enough damage to decide the outcome of the war, without having been hit by a retaliatory strike. This is what is meant by "the temptation of the first strike"; or, in more learned language, "strategic instability."

In the foregoing discussion I have simplified a real situation that is much more complex. (Thus it does not take into account underwater or concealed launch sites, and much else.) But it is nonetheless clear that MIRVs increase the complexity of the already difficult problem of eliminating the danger of a nuclear-missile war. In 1968 I said almost the same thing about ABM systems.* Since then the situation has become even more complicated.

Thermonuclear warfare has already become a dark reality of modern times, part of our lives, like Auschwitz, the Gulag, and famine. Perhaps I feel this more acutely

* See the footnote on page 67.

than many people, since for over twenty years I was in close contact with that fantastically terrifying world. Although since 1968 I have not had the necessary clearance to participate in secret work, and although my technical knowledge is of course obsolete, the psychological experience of those tense decades is still alive in me. And I feel this entitles me, and in fact obliges me, to put my thoughts in writing—perhaps controversially, but in any case frankly. Not for one moment can I forget that all this time hundreds of thousands of workers, thousands of talented engineers, and scientists from many fields of specialization are working on expanding and perfecting systems for the kind of attacks that are most difficult to ward off—with synchronized bombardments from thousands of MIRVed missiles with multimegaton warheads and decoys—and on creating complex and expensive defense systems serving similar military purposes.

In November 1955 important tests were carried out on a thermonuclear weapon. (In the course of those tests, two tragic events took place: a young soldier was killed when he was blown into a trench; and a two-year-old girl, the daughter of a German widow, died when a beam in a bomb shelter collapsed.) The evening after the test, at a private banquet attended only by the officials in charge of the tests, I proposed a toast that "our handiwork would never explode over cities." The director of the tests, a high-ranking general, felt obliged to respond with a parable. Its gist was that the scientists' job is to improve a weapon; how it is used is none of their business. Actually he anticipated what Khrushchev said several years later, at greater length, at a meeting with scientists in the Kremlin. (I have written about this previously.)

But I believed then, as I do now, that no one can shed his share of responsibility for something upon which the existence of mankind depends.

IV

Indochina and the Middle East

The tragic dangers of the disunity and nearsighted selfishness of the Western nations and of their underestimating the guile of their totalitarian enemies, which were described in the humanitarian and diplomatic problems discussed in the preceding chapters, have played a fatally prominent role in the military dramas of Indochina, the Middle East, and other trouble spots on the planet.

This past spring the world press headlined the tragedy of the millions of Vietnamese and Cambodian refugees fleeing from the Communist forces; about exhausted children; about columns of women, children, and old men mowed down by mortar fire; about planes taking off from surrounded airfields crowded with people who were crazed with fear. Now the Communists have won a complete victory in South Vietnam and Cambodia. Laos and Thailand may be next in line.

From Cambodia, where the victors—the Khmer Rouge—are not concealing their pro-Chinese orientation, we are already receiving gruesome reports of mass executions. (Where are those people who protested the excesses of Pinochet in Chile?) We are hearing of the unprecedented act of forced resettlement, from the towns to the countryside, of each and every one of the millions of townsmen and refugees, including dying people, patients prepared for operations, mothers about to give birth, and newborn children. One of the Thai ministers recently stated that many of those who had voluntarily returned to Cambodia were immediately executed.

In South Vietnam, order has been established after the model of North Vietnam: with pictures of Ho Chi Minh at every step; with rigid discipline and organization; and with a certain respectability. (Or the semblance of it. There have been reports of some self-immolations.) We may be sure that the population of South Vietnam is still faced with many years of ordeals—ordeals which, so far, no Communist country has been spared: cultural revolutions, massive repressions, and the dominance of the bureaucracy. The situation is complicated by the inevitable struggle between the USSR and China for influence in Vietnam—a struggle for whose "object" a high price will have to be paid.

What happened? As we know, in the 1960's strong opposition arose in the United States against American participation in the Vietnamese war—especially among the intellectuals. As recently as the late 1950's, it had seemed natural to the majority to aid an ally against open aggression, and the recent war in Korea stimulated hopes of a relatively easy victory. But ten years later it had become clear that the Korean analogy was deceptive. This war in the impenetrable jungles and rice paddies against an elusive, splendidly organized, ruthless, and selfless enemy, equipped with the newest Soviet weapons, had a very different look from the brilliant, lightning-fast operation at Inchon in 1950. The war became more and more hopeless, and increasingly cruel on both sides. Death came to tens of thousands of Americans and hundreds of thousands of Vietnamese— including civilians. South Vietnamese society, nominally democratic, in fact turned out to be (to a considerable extent) corrupt, under a military and police bureaucracy. (It may be that my information has caused me to be unjust on this point.)

The American critics of the Vietnamese war saw clearly that victory was not coming any closer, and they concluded (mistakenly, I believe) that it could be gained only through the kind of decisive actions that would jeopardize the entire modern world order. In short, they regarded the war as lost, and sought a more or less honorable way out of it, trying to stop the bombing, the killing of peaceful inhabitants by means of napalm, phosphorus, antipersonnel bombs, and the other infernal inventions of modern warfare, and to halt the deaths of American soldiers.

Here I am speaking of the most honest and historically responsible critics of the war (among whom I would include Daniel Ellsberg, the Berrigan brothers, Paul Mayer, and others). Along with them, there was a whole army of noisier, irresponsible critics who exploited the great tragedy for their own narrowly political ends. Especially disgraceful was the position of many Europeans, who did not lift a finger to provide any real help but often demagogically distorted the real, complex situation and the historical perspective.

Many who criticized United States participation in the Vietnam war overlooked the fact that the war had been started as a result of a direct military violation of the Geneva agreements; that during all those years there had been a large-scale military, economic, and political intervention by the USSR and China—not just altruistic aid but direct pressure; and that in fact the war and communism had been foisted upon the majority of the South Vietnamese and Cambodians without the right to choose and compare. They overlooked the fact that atrocities were committed by both sides. (In particular, they "didn't notice" such horrible things as the mass executions of thousands of people during the short-lived occupation of Hue by the North Vietnamese, the systematic abduction from villages of persons who had purportedly collaborated with the enemy, done little to help the partisans, etc.) They did not take into account the tremendous importance, in the matter of preserving good faith throughout the anti-Communist world, of America's living up to its commitments to its allies.

I believe that the tragic unfolding of events could have been prevented if the United States had acted more resolutely and consistently in the military and, especially, the political spheres. Political pressure on the USSR to prevent deliveries of arms to North Vietnam, the prompt dispatch of a large expeditionary force, involving the UN, more effective economic aid, and bringing in other Asian and European countries—these things could have influenced the course of events and thereby prevented the long war, with all its horrors on both sides.

A great share of the responsibility must be borne by the other Western countries, Japan, and the nations of the Third World, which in no way supported the ally that was helping them tremendously in the difficult, almost hopeless attempt to oppose the totalitarian threat in Southeast Asia. But then that which is today menacing Thailand may become (although in different forms) the fate of the whole world tomorrow.

I shall not even discuss the responsibility of the USSR, the People's Republic of China, and other socialist countries. Though in fact what should détente be if not, first of all, an attempt to avoid military conflicts?

Even when the war had reached an impasse, a combination of diplomatic and resolute military efforts, explained to the American people and to the whole world, could have stabilized the situation—just as it was stabilized in Europe, where the division of Germany is a tragic (and, I hope, temporary) phenomenon but not one that threatens international peace.

But all this proved impossible without the support of world and American public opinion. The Paris agreements resulted in the release, even before the war was over, of American POWs from imprisonment in North Vietnam. At the same time those agreements betrayed

South Vietnam, and, perhaps in the future, other nations of the world.

At a crucial moment and with no hesitation, the North Vietnamese, armed with the newest Soviet weapons, violated their obligations under the Paris agreements and overwhelmed the South Vietnamese Army. The result is common knowledge.

The last straw was provided by the protests in the United States against acceptance of Vietnamese refugees, who allegedly might be a burden upon the richest country in the world. This shameful final act of the drama was enlightening as to what depths of selfishness —of surfeited indifference to a great tragedy—can co-exist with the heroism of the American sailors and pilots who rescued refugees from the inferno of Vietnam; and with the high-mindedness of those families ready to take in Vietnamese children.

I want to believe that the terrible lesson of Indochina will not be lost upon the whole world—and especially not on America. Instead of isolationism, a selfless, generous, and courageous concern for the fates of all human beings. In place of illusions, a sober understanding of the challenge that history has thrown out to the leaders of the Western world. Not a half-hearted, inconsistent foreign policy never adequately explained to the public, but a carefully weighed choice of key ideas and a maximum of resolve in carrying them out. Not squabbles between political parties and petty economic and political calculations, but a readiness to make the necessary sacrifices—(and practice some austerity) for the sake of saving mankind and, thereby, one's own country. One should expect as much from the land of

Lincoln, Franklin Roosevelt, Eisenhower, and George Marshall, as well as from other countries in both the West and the East.

Another scene of bloody events is the Middle East. The decades of confrontation there—which, beginning in the 1950's was kindled by a self-seeking Soviet foreign policy—have so muddled the situation that it is now difficult to find a solution that is generally acceptable.

I often recall a talk given in 1955 by a high official of the USSR Council of Ministers to a group of scientists assembled at the Kremlin. He said that at that time (in connection with a trip to Egypt by D. T. Shepilov, a member of the Central Committee Presidium) the principles of the new Soviet policy in the Middle East were being discussed in the Presidium. And he observed that the long-range goal of that policy, as it had been formulated, was to exploit Arab nationalism in order to create difficulties for the European countries in obtaining crude oil, and thereby to gain influence over them. Today, when the world economy has been disorganized by the oil crisis, one can plainly see how crafty and effective is the subtext of the oil policy ("defending the just cause of the Arab nations")—although the West pretends that the USSR has played no role in the situation.

During the October War of 1973, begun by Egypt and Syria, General Sharon's armored divisions, which had broken through into a broad strategic area, were halted and brought back, owing to the intervention of Secretary of State Kissinger, who was in contact with the worried Soviet leaders. There is current an opinion holding that under those specific conditions the intervention was almost a betrayal of Israel's security, depriving it of the fruits of a hard-won victory. I do not fully share that view. But I feel that in October 1973 the United States and the European nations assumed responsibility for the fate of Israel, and that the time has come to pay that bill.

I believe that here, as in other, analogous problem areas, unity among the Western countries is indispensable. They must be ready to make economic sacrifices, up to and including a temporary embargo on Arabian oil; to demand firmly of the Soviet Government and other states that they stop or restrict deliveries of weapons; strive for a compromise, taking the real requirements of both sides into account. Only such a policy corresponds to the long-term interests of all countries in the world, including the Western nations.

One of the central problems of the Middle Eastern conflict is the fate of the Palestinian people. I am convinced that the interested parties—the Palestinian Arabs, Israel, Jordan—will undoubtedly find a solution acceptable to all. But it is important that the leaders of the Palestinians demonstrate their good faith toward the future regulation of the Arab-Israeli conflict as a whole and toward the security of Israel; and that they show their respect for international law, divorcing themselves from extremist and terrorist groups.

Another consequence of the Soviet presence in the Middle East is the tragedy of the Kurds in Iraq, which is in many ways analogous to the horrible fate of the

Ibos in Nigeria, for which Soviet intervention is also partially responsible. Iraq, after receiving tremendous military aid from the USSR—planes, tanks, missiles, napalm, military specialists, and access to data from reconnaissance satellites—turned all these things against a peaceable, proud people that wanted only autonomy within Iraq. I twice appealed to the Secretary General of the UN and the General Assembly for intervention: the first time with a view to alleviating the horrors of the war and stopping deliveries of foreign weapons; the second time in an attempt to secure the presence, in Kurdistan, of foreign observers so as to prevent excesses of vengeance by the victors. I still feel that there should be international intervention in, and attention to, the events in Iraqi Kurdistan.

The situation in many other parts of the world is also alarming. One of the most tragic problems is the lot of political prisoners in Indonesia. In 1974, acting on reliable information furnished me by members of the Soviet branch of Amnesty International, I appealed to the President of Indonesia to grant amnesty to the political prisoners. Unfortunately, that appeal has not yet been answered. That problem, and many others analogous to it (apartheid in the Republic of South Africa—one more flagrant example) must of course not be forgotten by the international community. The role of Amnesty International in all such matters has traditionally been great and generous. The international campaign against torture which this organization has launched is especially deserving of support.

V

The Liberal Intelligentsia of the West:
ITS ILLUSIONS
AND RESPONSIBILITIES

In recent years I have had occasion, for the first time, to meet people from the West—to verify and supplement my vicarious impressions of that world, which in so many respects forms a contrast with ours but which, in what is deepest and most important, is humanly understandable.

My attitude toward the foreign intelligentsia—toward the people I have come to know personally—is compounded of a deep liking, hope, and a respect bordering almost upon envy. In the best people from the West I see—and value very highly—an inner freedom, a readiness to debate combined with complete respect for the opinions of others, an absence of national prejudices, a realistic and practical cast of mind, and a readiness to undertake good works.

And yet in my opinion there is one characteristic common to many Western intellectuals that is somewhat disturbing. I refer to what I have called, in my own mind, "leftist-liberal faddishness." In a naïve form it is partially illustrated by a reply made by one American in a conversation with an emigrant from the USSR: "Well, all right. There are lots of things in Russia that you don't like. *You were mistreated there.* I can understand that. But I imagine you don't have any prejudices against China. Aren't you happy with what's going on there now?"

If my analysis and opinions are mistaken, I hope my friends in the West will forgive my lack of information. But if I have hit the mark even partially, then I believe they should take serious note.

I have no doubts as to the altruism and humanity of most of the Western liberal intellectuals—as to their hopes for the welfare of all people, for equal justice for all. But I fear that such things as a lack of information or the opportunity to analyze it critically, faddishness (which is all-powerful in the West), the fear of seeming old-fashioned (especially to one's own children, as many frankly admit), a lack of imagination where the factor of distance is involved, and an inadequate notion of the tragic complexity of real life (in particular, life in the socialist countries)—that these things may lead, and are already leading, to dangerous mistakes both in the intrapolitical life of the Western countries and in evaluating the difficult questions of international relations. Distance can cause one to have doubts about the strange and frightful things that one has learned only from books and stories.*

The liberal intellectuals of the West undoubtedly have good reasons for being dissatisfied with many aspects of their society. In hundreds of newspapers they read of acts of violence and cruelty, of social and racial discrimination, of the horrors of famine in the under-developed countries, and the terrors of war. They not only read these reports but see them with their own eyes, since there is no problem about traveling through their own country, or obtaining visas for Africa or Latin America.

People in the West enjoy a plethora of accessible information, an abundance of different ideas, and the co-existence of competing political groups. Some of these groups pursue very private interests, but all of them profess some brand of politics. In the West, political activity—the circulation and promotion of social ideas—becomes a profession just as easily as any other kind of activity, and is associated with the material interests of groups and individuals.

As is the case with us, many Westerners find themselves unable on their own to evaluate critically the flood of facts, opinions, and ideas that pours down upon them; and faddishness with all its irrational laws comes

---

* My wife's mother, who spent many years in Stalin's labor camps as a ChSIR (member of a traitor's family), has a close relative who lives in France (and who, incidentally, is a member of the French Communist Party). He once tried to find out from her whether there was "a particle of truth" in what Solzhenitsyn had written. She could only laugh bitterly.

to the fore. Often it is not the more logical ideas that take precedence but ephemeral notions that are more extravagant and easier to grasp.

"Left-wing faddishness," it seems to me, is now dominant in the West and has achieved that position through the complex interplay of various factors. Two of these are the eternal hankering of youth after the most radical changes and the fear of the more experienced and cautious representatives of the older generation that they may lag behind their own children. In the West, as everywhere else, there exist complex social problems that cannot be solved immediately, within the framework of the existing system. But radical solutions, with their persuasive, surface simplicity, create the illusion that those problems can be quickly solved.

Another important factor in the dominance of leftist faddishness is the fact that over a period of decades the Western world of free competition among ideas has constantly been fed by a small stream of pro-Soviet or pro-Chinese propaganda in which various, basically sound socialist ideas are tendentiously mixed with half-truths and out-and-out lies. This factor is perhaps not terribly important. But it, too, exerts a force; and in many ways it is rather effectively strengthened by the direct and indirect support of certain writers and politicians.

Such, it seems to me, is the soil that has given rise to the dominant stereotype of the leftist liberal intellectual of the West, with all his illusions and mistakes. Basically, however, the majority of such people have an outlook that is high-minded and humane, have real grounds for dissatisfaction with their society and feel good will and an aspiration toward justice and the common weal. And this permits me to hope that in the final analysis the Western intellectual won't let the rest of us down. Totalitarianism, fascism of whatever brand, demagogues, and intriguing politicians—these things are not, I trust, for the likes of him.

With respect to his own country, the Western liberal intellectual supports the full measure of civil liberties and economic and social reforms of the socialist type. These aspirations are in fact in the spirit of the times; and if they are realized cautiously, they will probably promote justice, happiness, and the flourishing of society, and help to eliminate rough spots and societal defects.

It is not by chance that I emphasize caution. I am deeply convinced that the thoughtless, frivolous pursuit of leftist-liberal faddishness is fraught with great dangers. On the international level, one danger is the loss of Western unity and of a clear understanding of the ever-constant global threat posed by the totalitarian nations. The West must not under any circumstances allow the weakening of its stand against totalitarianism. There is an internal danger for each country of slipping into state-capitalist totalitarian socialism. These two threats are of course closely related. And the growth of leftist ideas must not lead to a weakening of the international defense of human rights throughout the world, with the same standards for the Englishman, the Frenchman, the Black from the Republic of South Africa, the Crimean Tatar, the Russian, the Ukrainian, the Italian, and the

Vietnamese. In comparison with these problems, many of the day-to-day matters that are disturbing the ordinary man in the West are of slight significance. If he, his children, or his grandchildren ever live under a system even remotely resembling ours or the Chinese, they will understand—it isn't too late.

The late Arkady Belinkov,° who was received with so much coolness and distrust in the West, once wrote to the PEN Club:† "Socialism is the kind of thing it's easy to sample but hard to spit out." And indeed, by virtue of its inherent qualities of immanent stability, and the inertia of fear and passivity, totalitarian socialism (which may be called "pseudosocialism") is a kind of historical dead end from which it is troublesome to escape.

Certain Westerners have expressed the opinion that the failures and calamities in the USSR and the other Eastern socialist nations are due to the fact that these are "benighted Asian countries" without democratic traditions and without any history of respect for the rights of the individual. For these nations—for the Russians, the Chinese, the Vietnamese—everything that takes place (terrorism, muddling, dirt in the maternity home, violations of freedoms—I am intentionally citing disparate things) is allegedly customary and even "progressive," since those people have such a strange way of taking a step forward. But, it is alleged, the West, with

° A Soviet literary critic and former political prisoner who defected in 1968 and died in the United States in 1970 after open-heart surgery. [Translator]

†An international writers' organization. [Translator]

its democratic traditions, will rise in one upward swoop to the higher level of "socialism with a human face"—humane and effective. In particular, such arguments are, I gather, widespread among the Western Communists—especially among the intellectuals and leaders. But for the rank-and-file Communists they employ the simpler methods of distorting and concealing the truth about the lands of victorious socialism.

These typically leftist-liberal arguments (I call them "inverted Slavophilism") are in no way justified by historical experience. To me they represent a dangerous illusion and an immoral use, perhaps in order to appease consciences, of different yardsticks for "our people" and "other people."

Heretofore socialism has always meant a one-party system, power in the hands of a grasping and incompetent bureaucracy, the expropriation of all private property, terrorism on the part of the Cheka or its counterparts, the destruction of productive forces, with their subsequent restoration and expansion at the cost of countless sacrifices by the people, and violence done to free consciences and convictions. So it has been in the USSR, in the people's democracies, in the People's Republic of China, and in Cuba. (The example of Yugoslavia, the nation most independent of Soviet guardianship and the freest and most open of the socialist countries, is especially significant.)

Is all this inevitable? I believe that in principle "socialism with a human face" is possible, and represents a high form of social organization. But it is possible only as a result of extraordinary collective efforts, plus wisdom and selflessness exercised by a great part of the people—something uniformly difficult to achieve for any country, requiring especially favorable domestic and foreign conditions. The total nationalization of all means of production, the one-party system, and the repression of honest convictions—all must be avoided or totalitarianism will prevail.

I would also assume that the totalitarian states stand at an especially great distance from this ideal; that they are farther from it than capitalist states of the West. In 1968, the world witnessed an attempt by the Czechoslovak Communists, supported by the Czech people—especially the intelligentsia and the working class—to purge totalitarian socialism of its monstrosities (it was there that the phrase "socialism with a human face" came into use) and, at the same time, to rid the country of the USSR's humiliating and dangerous guardianship. This attempt achieved certain successes, and elicited admiration throughout the world. But it was precisely the successes that made the USSR, East Germany, and Poland fear them as dangerous examples, and that served as the reason for the shameful intervention. Totalitarianism defended itself with tanks; but in so doing it compromised socialist ideas in the eyes of millions of people for a long time.

The dangers of totalitarianism associated with the socialist, so-called progressive path of development—especially in the specifically modern setting of a divided world—have been repeatedly and glaringly evident in recent times.

As I write, the world is watching Portugal, where the

mechanics of falling into totalitarianism are in operation. Although apparently enjoying the support of Moscow, the Portuguese Communist Party was defeated in the April 1975 elections. After the voting it began to shove its rivals around, using the same unceremonious methods of demagogy, provocation, police tyranny, and blackmail that its forerunners employed in the past: in 1917, 1933, and 1948.

The trend toward totalitarianism of the military-socialist type can also be detected in certain non-Communist circles of the "Armed Forces Movement." Especially sinister is the growing influence on society exercised by the secret police: a "state within a state," a twentieth-century *oprichnina*,* like the NKVD in the Stalin Era. Apparently, the Communists play an especially large role in the Portuguese secret police. One would hope that, for all this, the Portuguese people have learned something from the history of other countries and will avoid the fate with which they are threatened. The world community must do everything possible to help them avoid tragedy.†

The manifestations of the leftist position in international relations are no less serious. The illusions commonly entertained by the leftist-liberal intelligentsia as to the nature of society in the USSR and the other socialist countries, as to real domestic and geopolitical

---

* The "private household" or "bodyguard" of Ivan the Terrible. *Inter alia,* Ivan employed this terrorist organization in his campaign against the boyars. [Translator]

† Dr. Sakharov wrote these paragraphs about the fluid situation in Portugal in the early summer of 1975. [Publisher's note]

aims of the ruling circles in those countries, make it difficult to evaluate the true significance of détente. And sometimes governments of the Western countries are prompted to take false and dangerous positions—to grant unilateral concessions and "gifts" in the course of détente. In the Western nations, the majority opinion has a direct influence on the practical actions of political leaders, who (so it seems to me, looking at them from here) usually pay heed to their constituents, the press, and public opinion.

In particular, the leftist intellectuals are urging their governments toward unilateral disarmament. But such disarmament could lead to a disturbance of the international equilibrium—to weakening the Western position vis-à-vis the totalitarian threat—and could induce stepped-up expansion by the socialist nations, especially in the strategically important focal points of the Third World; e.g., the Indian Ocean.

The domestic socioeconomic problems of the Western countries should be solved by mobilizing resources and by means of temporary economic belt-tightening—not at the cost of weakening their stand toward the threat. Balanced disarmament is extremely important; but this result cannot be achieved from a position of weakness.

Also important is the political and economic unification of the Western countries, as in the Common Market (of course not by opposing the United States, the leader of the Western world, but in close cooperation with it). I experienced a feeling of relief at the outcome of the 1975 Common Market referendum in Britain, and of Greece's impending adherence to the Council of Europe. In these situations, the immediate economic aspect of the problem must be relegated to a secondary status. It is most important to oppose expansion by the totalitarian countries. So far, the leftist, "progressive" forces have not taken a clear-cut position in all these matters. The "leftist" mistakes in Vietnam have been repeated in other cases as well. The leftist-liberal intellectuals are often ready to support and defend extremist and even terrorist groups in their own countries and throughout the world, if these groups are using a leftist mask, while at the same time the intellectuals are ready to condemn harshly those who do not make common cause with them for being conservative and reactionary. This viewpoint is a tremendous danger to mankind.

I will conclude this chapter with a discussion of the defense of human rights throughout the world—especially in the socialist countries, where they are too often ignored. The leftists usually accept too trustingly the dogma of the advantages of the socialist system, and avoid listening to anything that contradicts it. Some of them still do not want to believe the evidence of frightful events in the past presented in such books as Robert Conquest's *The Great Terror*, Solzhenitsyn's *Gulag Archipelago*, Roy Medvedev's *Let History Judge*, and other historical works. Reports of current social and economic difficulties and the political, ethnic, and religious persecutions that are taking place today are often regarded by such intellectuals as exaggerated and artificially selective.

But even in the most hideous years of Stalin's terrorism, when the fog of misinformation and pro-Soviet propaganda was especially thick, there were honest and brave individuals in the West who realized the truth and managed to speak it. Today the situation has changed in many respects; the fog has begun to lift. The Twentieth Party Congress, the events in Hungary and Czechoslovakia, the Cultural Revolution and the Great Leap Forward in China, the wars in Korea and Vietnam, and the events in the Middle East, Portugal, Chile, and Cuba—all these episodes have been influential.

Individual actions taken in socialist countries have played a special role in leading to important psychological shifts. Each deed of this kind is pursued at a high price. In some cases a person involved may suffer repression; in other situations there may be long-term consequences for the cause he has espoused, for his friends, his children, or his close relatives. I cited *supra* many examples of such repressions in the USSR. There has been considerable attention focused on the fate of the writer Mihajlo Mihajlov, convicted in Yugoslavia for his bold public statements, including speaking out in my defense.[*]

---

[*] Addressing myself directly to the Western intelligentsia, I want to say the following: I cannot but feel that the arrests of my close friends, Sergei Kovalev and Andrei Tverdokhlebov, were to some extent due to their closeness to me. The same thing applies to the persecution of Valentin Turchin, Yury Orlov, and Lydia Chukovskaya. (She spoke out in my defense in 1973 and in early 1974 was expelled from the Writers' Union.) The pressure on members of my family, who have become hostages, is further evidence of the same tactic. Right now, in publishing this essay, I am thinking not only of the serious and much-needed discussions of its content but of various ensuing surprises that may come from quite another direction:

Today, in the age of the technological revolution, the intelligentsia is, along with the working class, the most socially conscious and influential segment of society. A great deal depends upon how clear-cut and well-founded its views are; upon the absence of illusions about those views; upon how well-organized the intelligentsia is; and upon its impartiality. I would hope that my book will be heeded and will prove useful. I am hoping, in particular, that members of the Western intelligentsia will more vigorously defend human rights in our nation and the other socialist nations: the right to the free choice of one's country of residence; the rights of the ethnic minorities—the Crimean Tatars, the Germans, the Lithuanians, the Estonians, the Latvians, the Ukrainians, and many others; the rights of persecuted religious groups; the right to defense on the part of prisoners of conscience—such individuals as Mihajlov in Yugoslavia, Leonid Plyushch, Vladimir Bukovsky, Valentin Moroz, Kronid Lyubarsky, the Dzhemilev brothers, Anatoly Chinnov, and hundreds of others. (I have written about some of them in detail in other published statements.)

In 1974 international support saved the Panovs, the

-----

in the form of newspaper articles by my colleagues in the Academy of Sciences, threats from pseudo-Christians [In December 1974 Dr. Sakharov received a threatening letter from the so-called Russian Christian Party. See also the *Chronicle of Human Rights in the USSR*, No. 11/12, page 20, (Translator)], or something even worse. People from the West often ask how they can help me. But sometimes, when I say, "By helping my friends," they seem rather puzzled. This, too, evinces a kind of illusion—an underestimation of the characteristics of our society.

ballet dancers who had been trying to obtain permission to emigrate to Israel. At that time, famous actors and dancers demonstrated in front of the Soviet embassy in London. Stagehands and actors boycotted the tour of the Bolshoi, jeopardizing both the pocketbook and prestige of the Soviet system—its two Achilles' heels. Unquestionably, the public statement by Prime Minister Harold Wilson played a decisive role, bringing the protests up into those high quarters not usually reached by noise from the street.

But after all, the same thing is possible in other cases. The story of the Panovs confirms that only the strongest pressure—the kind to which the Soviet authorities are most vulnerable—has any chance of success. Only pressure can compel those officials who are not entitled to deviate from their instructions to request further instructions from the higher leadership, which is sometimes capable of reacting in an unconventional way.

Conclusion

In "Thoughts on Progress . . . ," "Memorandum," and other essays, I offered several proposals for essential domestic reforms in our country, and for desirable changes in international relations, and called for the international defense of human rights.

Most of those ideas were by no means original. I have already indicated that they derived from statements by others in the postwar years. Later, the same ideas were restated in many articles and speeches published abroad and in *samizdat*. During all these years I never received any response from the Soviet leaders to my proposals; and indeed, I did not expect any reaction. But I still believe such attempts are useful—not only as the most concise exposition of one's views and aspirations but as a needed alternative to official positions.

What internal reforms, then, seem to me necessary in

order to bring our country out of a constant state of general crisis, and to eliminate the consequent danger to mankind? (The same thing applies, by and large, to the other socialist countries.)

One. Broadening the economic reform of 1965 (which, as is known, has been rolled back to an earlier stage of implementation); full autonomy for plants, factories, etc., in matters of economics, production, and personnel policy.

Two. Partial denationalization of all types of economic and societal activity, probably excluding heavy industry, major transportation, and communications. Partial denationalization is especially critical in the area of services (repair shops, hotels, restaurants, etc.), in retail trade, and in education and medical care. In agriculture we must have partial decollectivization and government encouragement of the private sector as the most productive and the one best able to help restore social and psychological health to the rural areas, now under the threat of a complete lapse into drunkenness and torpor. Ever since the historical rise of settled, agricultural communities, working the land has been—for millions of people—not just a means of livelihood but something which endowed life with an inner meaning. During the era of collectivization, that "something" was barbarously destroyed; and among those who possessed it, the most viable were physically annihilated. But we must hope that spirit will be regenerated if suitable conditions arise.

Conclusion

Three. Full amnesty for all political prisoners, including inmates of special psychiatric hospitals, and all persons convicted for their religious beliefs, national aspirations, and attempts to leave the country. Alleviating the lot of prisoners of all categories; elimination of forced labor; abolishing restrictions on nutrition, visits, mailings, and receipt of parcels; improving medical care; permitting the sending of medication by mail. Making all places of confinement accessible to international observers. Abolishing capital punishment. Giving amnesty to all those who have been imprisoned for more than fifteen years.

Four. A law giving the freedom to strike.

Five. A series of legislative acts guaranteeing real freedom of convictions, freedom of conscience, and freedom to circulate information. Eliminating several articles of the Criminal Code that contradict the above principles.

Six. Legislation providing that the adoption of the most important decisions (both those international in scope and those of domestic socioeconomic and ecological significance) be publicly disclosed and subject to public accountability.

Seven. A law assuring the freedom to choose one's place of residence and of employment within the country.

Eight. Legislation guaranteeing the freedom to leave the country (emigration, or trips for one purpose or another) and to return to it.

Nine. Banning all forms of Party and official privileges not directly required by the performance of official duties. Equal rights for all citizens as a basic principle of the state.

Ten. Legislative confirmation of the right of Soviet republics to secede, and the right to discuss the question of secession.

Eleven. A multiparty system.

Twelve. Currency reform: the free exchange of rubles for foreign currency. Limitation of the foreign trade monopoly.

I regard these reforms as conditions precedent to gradually improving the social situation in the country, alleviating the material deficiencies of the majority of the working population, creating a moral climate of freedom, happiness, and good will; restoring values common to mankind that have been lost; and removing the danger that our country—as a closed, totalitarian police state armed with a superweapon and possessing tremendous means and resources—represents for the entire world.

I feel it necessary to emphasize that I am a confirmed evolutionist and reformist, and an opponent, as a matter of principle, of violent, revolutionary changes of the social order, which always lead to the destruction of the economic and legal systems, as well as to mass suffering, lawlessness, and horrors.

I have discussed the many alarming and tragic facts of the present international situation which testify to the West's essential weakness and disunity vis-à-vis the totalitarian challenge, of which the events in Indochina are the most dramatic example. The policy of the socialist countries has now taken on a more subtle character, with the preservation of most of the former domestic and foreign goals and the simultaneous introduction of new goals and forms of interacting with the outer world. Under these new conditions, what changes in the strategy and tactics of the West—and in the policy of the Third World countries—strike me as the most important?

One. Most pressing of all is the unity of the Western countries; a unified strategy for the entire expanding set of problems in relations with the socialist countries and those of the Third World. These include joint defense, trade agreements, defense of human rights, disarmament talks, granting of credits, economic assistance (foodstuffs in particular), aid in developing technology, environmental protection, settling postwar boundaries, eliminating military conflicts in the trouble spots, defending the freedom to exchange people and information.

Unity requires a leader. And that leader, both by right and by virtue of its great responsibilities, is the United States—economically, technologically, and militarily the most powerful of the Western countries.

A unified strategy cannot be based on particular and temporary interests; it must be far-reaching, firm, and altruistic. The close interdependence among the Western countries in matters of defense, economics, and politics will render impossible those depressing instances (all too frequent today) of betraying common interests for the sake of private ones. I have mentioned the lack of support in Western countries for the emigration amendment to the American trade bill, which was of worldwide humanitarian significance and important to the entire process of détente. Yet America's allies, while taking advantage of its economic and defense support, have not merely failed to form a common front but, on the contrary, are vying and competing with one another to help undermine the whole initiative.

I call upon the Western intelligentsia and international humanitarian organizations to promote the unity of the West in every possible way.

Two. As before (compare "Memorandum") I ask for the creation, under the aegis of the UN, of an International Consultative Committee of experts on juridical, social, and ecological problems, and on matters of disarmament, authorized to obtain from all governments, on an obligatory basis, replies to inquiries and to recommendations. I hope that the United States or some other nation will support this initiative at the UN General Assembly.

Conclusion

Three. As before, I call for a broader use of UN armed forces to quell armed conflicts (including those of an "internal" nature, as in Nigeria and in Iraqi Kurdistan).

Four. I emphasize the following principles in the area of disarmament:

a) An agreed-upon reduction of armaments to the same level of capacity for both sides at each stage of reduction, with the gradual and increasingly substantial reduction of that level.

This principle should be applied both to talks on limitations of strategic arms—in particular, the offensive thermonuclear missiles of the nuclear powers; and to regional discussion—especially between the Warsaw Pact countries and NATO.

b) The establishment of a perfected system of verification involving the use of inspection groups, including representatives of the other side and of international organizations, with free access to the entire territory of the country being inspected.

c) The introduction of international limitations on deliveries of weapons to other states. I attach special significance to this proposal. In my opinion, an agreed-upon reduction in deliveries of weapons to trouble spots like the Middle East is particularly important. Historical experience testifies to the fact that when cannons are at hand, they will sooner or later begin to shoot. The statesmen of the West must use all means of diplomacy—pressure and trade—to achieve that end. (If blood continues to flow, what is détente?)

d) Elimination of the technical factors contributing to the arms race. Discontinuing new development projects on the basis of a list that has been agreed upon. Relaxation of security regulations and, ultimately, agreement on the total prohibition of secret work. It is difficult to overestimate the importance of such a compact to the future of mankind.

e) Elimination of all factors contributing to strategic instability. Banning of MIRVs and limitations on ABM systems.

Five. A concern for greater openness in the socialist countries—for the freedom to exchange people and information—must be one of the central tasks of the coordinated policy of the Western countries. Western European nations have formulated this goal at the European security conference. But at present I fear they are not putting enough pressure on the socialist countries but are making it possible for the latter to make deals and, step by step, to obtain meaningless formulations that suit their purposes. In the meantime, I feel that the goals of the socialist countries (in particular, fixing the postwar boundaries) do not fully correspond to the interests of Europe's future—at any rate, pending the achievement of German unification. It is precisely the openness of the socialist countries, plus a balanced disarmament, that can guarantee the security of Europe and the whole world. It is particularly important that there be a free exchange of tourists, citizens going elsewhere for employment, to study, to get medical treatment, and to do scientific work on a free, popular basis and not in accordance with the slavish traditions of the Soviet visa office, personnel departments, the KGB, and others of their ilk. There must be free exchange of books, magazines and journals, newspapers, and films. It is essential to revoke the UN General Assembly's shameful banning of free television from satellites. (Hundreds of millions of people watch television, and they have the right to see what they want to.) It is also essential that foreign radio broadcasting to the USSR be expanded and improved, with a prohibition against all forms of jamming. In this connection, what is needed most is accurate, concise reporting of facts about politically important matters.

Six. Not only individuals but governments and international organizations must be concerned with defending human rights throughout the world, with the same criteria for all countries. In 1948 the Universal Declaration of Human Rights proclaimed the international character of the defense of human rights; but so far little has been done to implement that principle. The central problem is the free choice of one's country of residence. So long as that right is not permitted, one part of the world will remain a huge concentration camp threatening the other part.

Seven. The problem of relations with the Third World, where half of humankind lives, is of special importance. Comprehensive aid in the development of technology, in training key personnel, in the form of foodstuffs and other material assistance is now being carried out on a broad scale; but it is still not enough. This aid must be further expanded—in particular by the nations of Europe, the developed socialist countries, Japan, and the United States—which is bearing most of the burden. But on the other hand, the developing countries themselves must restructure their national psychologies in the direction of greater responsibility for their own fates. It is time they stopped blaming their misfortunes on colonialism and neocolonialism. Only creative energy, especially in the area of material production, can ensure their future. The oil-producing nations have a special responsibility. Since October 1973 there has been a speculative increase in the price of crude oil that has disorganized the world economy. Suffering has been particularly great in the developing countries, where millions have been faced with famine. It is essential to establish prices that do not destroy the world in which we are all living, together. This is in the interests of all, including the oil-producing nations.

One more observation—perhaps a tactless one. At the UN the Third World countries usually vote with the totalitarian states, thereby almost paralyzing that organization. But the UN is one of the few forces on which our common hopes for a better world are based. To wreck those hopes because of political games—because of temporary, narrowly national interests and prejudices—is unwise, to say the least.

I have written this book the way people build a modern building. Or rather, the way a rook builds its nest: first the frame, then the twigs that have been laid by. All the holes visible to the builder are filled in, but some unused twigs remain.

The reality of the contemporary world is complex,

with many planes. It is a fantastic mix of tragedy, irreparable misfortune, apathy, prejudices, and ignorance, plus dynamism, selflessness, hope, and intelligence. The future may be even more tragic. Or it may be more worthy of human beings—better and more intelligent. Or, again, it may not be at all. It depends on all of us—people living in the USSR, China, India, the United States, Egypt, Israel, Thailand, Italy, England, France, Japan, Australia, Holland, Germany, Syria, Vietnam, Iran—in every country of the world. It depends on our wisdom, our freedom from illusion and prejudices, our readiness to work, to practice intelligent austerity, and on our kindness and our breadth as human beings. That wisdom must be manifested in a genuine rapprochement among the countries of the First, Second, and the Third worlds; in overcoming disunity in the name of man and his rights. The future of intelligence, of scientific prediction and progress—the future of the common weal—must be realized.

Moscow, June 1975

A Note on the Type

The text of this book was set in Caledonia, a Linotype face designed by W. A. Dwiggins. It belongs to the family of printing types called "modern faces" by printers—a term used to mark the change in style of type letters that occurred about 1800. Caledonia borders on the general design of Scotch Modern, but is more freely drawn than that letter.

Composed, printed, and bound by
American Book–Stratford Press, Saddle Brook, New Jersey.